No Longer

*B*adruddin's journey to see
stani origin, who is Muslim-identified, poignantly resonates amongst many Diasporan lesbian and gay South Asians, whether from Pakistan, India, or Bangladesh. His story reflects so much of our own lives—our own struggles and pain. Through his eyes, we see the many layers of belonging and not belonging; of rejection and isolation; of denial and acceptance; of fear and desire to belong. We understand. We know because we have been there, are there, are going to be there sooner or later, or refuse to enter that personal quest.

His story exposes our own struggles and pain; the quest for love amidst a cultural framework that allows no (or very little) personal space and choice, that places a social compulsion for procreation above that of personal desire and inner longings; that captures the lives of so many males and females in hidden acts, behind locked doors, or behind dark bushes.

This is a story of courage too. As Stephen Murray points out in the afterward, Badruddin's opening of himself, a tearing away of the layers of invisibility and denial, is itself a challenge to Muslim orthodoxy and Pakistani culture. To be one's own witness in front of one's community is a "shocking" act of revelation. Hence the pseudonym. A saving grace, or a graceful saviour to family, friends and, community.

But the great danger exists in the current context of AIDS in South Asia, which as a region has the fastest rate of increase of HIV infections in the world. How can we address these hidden frameworks of sex, longing, belonging, and male-to-male desire? Must we see so many of our own people die from

AIDS because of this invisibility and denial? Die because we cannot or will not act? Die because "silence = death"?

Badruddin is no longer silent.

> Shivananda Khan
> Executive Director
> The Naz Foundation
> Palingswick House
> 241 King Street
> London W6 9LP
> England, UK

The Naz Foundation is an HIV/AIDS-prevention and sexual-health agency working with the South and West Asian communities.

Trikone[1] (Sanskrit for "triangle") is a nonprofit group for lesbian, gay, and bisexual South Asians. (South Asia includes Afghanistan, Bangladesh, Bhutan, Burma, India, Maldives, Nepal, Pakistan, Sri Lanka and Tibet.)

Trikone's brings women and men of South Asian heritage together in a friendly, supportive, and nonjudgmental environment, and promotes awareness, visibility, and acceptance of alternative sexuality in society. Trikone proudly affirms both South Asian identity as well as lesbian, gay, and bisexual sexualities. Founded in 1986 in the San Francisco Bay Area, Trikone is the oldest group of its kind in the world.

Trikone
P.O. Box 21354, San Jose, CA 95151-1354
E-mail: trikone@rahul.net
Web address: http://www.rahul.net/trikone
☎ (408) 270-8776

---

[1] *Tri* as in "trim," *kone* as in "cone."

SEX, LONGING & Not Belonging

Badruddin Khan

With an Afterword by Stephen O. Murray, Ph.D.

Except for brief passages quoted in its original English-language form in print or electronic media reviews, no part of this book may be reproduced in any form, or by any means, now known or hereafter invented, electronic or mechanical, including photocopying and recording or by any information-storage or retrieval system, nor may it be translated into any other language in whole or part, without the express written permission of the publisher.

Floating Lotus USA
P.O. Box 147
Oakland, CA 94604-0147
USA
☎ **(510) 465-0747**

Floating Lotus Communications Co., Ltd.
P.O. Box 44
Ratchawithi Post Office
Bangkok 10408, Thailand

Floating Lotus Books is an imprint of Floating Lotus Communications Co., Ltd. Floating Lotus and Bua Luang, and the Lai-Thai Man-in-the-Lotus logo are trademarks of Floating Lotus Communications Co., Ltd.

Cover and text design by Santiphap Chaiyana
Printed and bound in Thailand
Printed by Pyramid Printers ☎ [66] [02] 712-0199
First printing in 1997

Library of Congress Catalog Card Number 96-062080
ISBN 0-942777-16-6

Floating Lotus Books ‹floatinglotus@hotmail.com›
Copyright © 1997 by Badruddin Khan. All rights reserved.

BADRUDDIN KHAN is the *nom de plume* of a Canadian business consultant who was born and raised in Karachi, Pakistan.
Mr. Khan's E-mail address: ‹bkhan@hotmail.com›

STEPHEN O. MURRAY earned a Ph.D. in sociology from the University of Toronto and is the author or co-author of ten books, the most recent ones being *American Gay*, *Angkor Life*, and *Islamic Homosexualities*.

ॐ Contents ॐ

Introduction	5
My Early Days	14
Discovery	14
Karachi, The City	21
My Childhood and Family	30
Early Awakenings	38
Delicious Dalliances on the Home Front	41
The Painter's Helper	42
Tailored to Please	47
The Wayward Pathan	50
Action on the Sidelines: Kushti	53
Adolescence and a New Emergence	61
The Puzzling New World	72
Could I Be Gay?	75
The Virtuoso Seduction	83
Race and Racism	92
Greek Discoveries	98
Am I Muslim?	103
Return of the Expatriate	115
Paki-Bonding	116

Diddling the Natives	120
Creating a Safe Haven	126
Building and Managing a Stable	129
The Saga of Haider	132
A Fresh Start	**145**
Fulfilling My Duty	**153**
Choosing a Wife	156
Bride and Bridegroom	161
Cherry Picking	162
Married Life	164
California, Here I Come	**173**
Greg's Cadillac	177
Juan's Siren Song	181
The Taste of Love	198
Closets vs. "Mr. Right"	201
Family	**209**
Dick in Karachi	213
Afterword by Stephen O. Murray, Ph.D.	**220**

Introduction

I was born in 1951, four years after the creation of the Islamic Republic of Pakistan on 14 August, 1947, from what had previously been British India. My parents were Mohajirs;[1] that is, at the time of partition, they had fled from what is now predominantly Hindu India to become part of this new country. Pakistan in its early years was a fragile experiment and lacked even the basic institutions required for government. There was no banking system, organized military, or adequate health-care framework. Like many other Mohajirs for whom Pakistan represented a promised land with new opportunities, my parents, uncles, and other relatives devoted themselves to nation-building with commitment and purpose. The immigrant Mohajirs brought with them the secular sense of mission of ex

---

[1] Mohajir literally means "emigrant." It is used to identify the group of people that moved from India to Muslim Pakistan after partition of the Indian sub continent into Pakistan and India, in 1947. Karachi is in the Sind province of Pakistan, and local Sindhis have long resented the relative affluence of Mohajirs. This is one of the underlying flash points in the ethnic tensions in Karachi today.

patriates everywhere that allowed them to succeed by measures of wealth and power. This, today, is one of the underlying causes of civil tension in Karachi, where the native Sindhis are asserting claim to political dominance, as original natives of the area.

My immediate family was conservative in social manners, but intellectually free-thinking and open to new ideas. This was unusual in a country where most people are ill-educated, and where tradition is seen as the most reliable guide. My parents came from modest professional family backgrounds. They valued education highly for its own sake, well beyond any promise of material gain, although we always lived in comfortable, if somewhat threadbare, middle-class surroundings.

I emigrated to North America in my late teens, relatively naïve and sheltered. After a university education at Columbia University in New York City, I took a job in Toronto, Canada, and settled down in the professions. I "discovered" that I was gay in my early twenties, while an undergraduate. Rather, I discovered the label and concluded that it probably could be applied to me. However, it was more than a decade later, after a failed marriage, that I was able to identify with the term sufficiently to consider myself part of the "gay community." It took visits to San Francisco and Houston, away from the cultural connections of Toronto, for me to enter into what I consider in retrospect to be my first serious relationship with a man. Now, back in Toronto, and living a quiet life in suburbia with my lover, Dick, I have managed a transition to a life that is more holistic, better integrated, and with some semblance of balance between love and work.

Before my "coming out," the only communities that mattered were professional, Pakistani, or Muslim. In North America in the 1980s and 1990s, it is necessary to wear a "label-identifier" in order to associate with a community, and necessary to associate with a community in order to have a sense of belonging. In this relatively egalitarian milieu, affiliations can be switched, alliances can be upgraded, and meaningful relationships entered and exited in the course of a day. To customize my new home to suit me, to belong, I therefore had to address the question of sexual identity in the context of being a gay Muslim. My attempt to answer this question has spanned over fifteen years, not all of which has been constructive or productive. During this journey I have despaired in introspective self-pity, celebrated in gay marches, and often pondered the purpose of my life, away from the heterosexual family model. My journey continues to this day.

None of these issues mattered, and none of these questions arose, while I was growing up in Pakistan. I *belonged*, had a predetermined place, and an array of reasonable social options ahead of me. These options would not preclude an ongoing but discreet same-sex relationship, or even multiple concurrent same-sex relationships. However, all these options assumed marriage as at least a cultural anchor and social cover. The raising of a family was the natural reason to strive to achieve success, and the sole path to happiness.

Pakistan is a predominantly Muslim country. However, Islam is remarkably modern in its moralizing about sexual expression; some *imams* and *mullahs*,[1] though, are far more restrictive in their interpretive prescriptions. The religion itself appears to consider it normal and healthy for men to be sexual, as long as it does not interfere with their role as future heads of families, and as

---

[1] *Imams* and *mullahs* manage mosques and organize and lead religious congregations. Sunni Islam, which is the dominant denomination in Pakistan, does not have a formal class of priests with hierarchically derived powers.

long as it is not proscribed sexual contact. Once a man grows up and is considered socially ready, Islam prescribes marriage. This is necessary since men have social roles, and responsibilities to their families and communities to be role models. Although forbidden and rarely discussed except by renegade poets, sex between men, between men and boys, and between boys is not uncommon in Muslim countries. Such an infraction does not count as much as illicit sex between unmarried men and women, which directly threatens the family unit. Emotional attachment between males is acceptable and even romanticized in song and verse, but is considered as merely "training wheels" on which to practice for the real thing: marriage and procreation.

After marriage, while monogamy is not required, it is lauded. Extramarital relationships are tolerated, as long as they are kept quiet and do not threaten the family unit. Ironically, since the threat to family is more tangible if such affairs involve potentially marriageable women who might bear children, discreet male-male affairs are less a cause for concern than male-female affairs. Discreet male-male affairs are not relevant to society.

Because no kind of sex is openly discussed in the conservative culture of Pakistan, extramarital sex practices cannot be said to be "acceptable." They just happen and are known to happen. Similarly, there are those who will deny that any same-sex relationships occur, other than out of "necessity," as in prisons. Some deny the existence of serious same-sex relationships that reflect a differentiated identity in a country like Pakistan, but they are wrong. What is true is that the sensibility underlying such an identity is almost always sublimated, because, while there is plenty of homosexual sex, there can be no gay social or political identity. Such a movement would threaten the primacy of family, and would be instantly squashed or marginalized.

Only *gandus*[1] seek sex with men, and such men are not respectable.

I am not a scholar of Islam, and so my interpretation of Islamic rules concerning sex is based purely on my limited observations and reading. Others may disagree with me, in which case my comments may serve to initiate dialog, and I am ready to stand corrected should I have made mistakes in interpretation. For any errors, I apologize in advance. I am a Muslim to this day and do not intend any disrespect. I go to Eid prayers at the local mosque, even Friday prayers on occasion, and I mix and mingle with other Muslims in the community who are from a wide range of backgrounds in the melting pot of Toronto. At the same time, since I live with a male lover, I am clearly "gay" in the North American and European sense of the word. I lead a conservative, "normal" life in every sense of the word, attempting to maintain it with high moral and ethical standards. I also know of other Muslims who are gay. Why am I writing this book, instead of remaining silent? My reasons are complex, and I am not sure I myself completely understand this desire to speak out, but one key motivation is to describe my long and weary journey to self-acceptance, so that others may benefit, and feel less alone. I know Pakistanis and Muslims who fall into the same category as I do, and this book is to tell them that they are not alone. In the end it is for God to decide whether I belong in heaven or hell for who I am and whether speaking the truth about myself is brave or sinful.

I also had to decide whether or not to include explicit sexual content into the book, and I hope the reader will agree that I chose the middle path. To limit myself to just describing sexual

---

[1] The term *gandu* is pejorative and refers primarily to men who engage in receptive anal sex.

encounters, ultimately, would have been boring, and there is an ample supply of such material already available by writers more skillful than I. At the same time, my sexuality is an integral part of my identity, and to sterilize my life by avoiding any discussion of sex would have been absurd. I make no apologies for being a sexual animal. I neither celebrate it nor do I feel shamed by it. This is the way I am—normal and probably very average by most measures. It is, however, the fire of sexual desire that kindled my search for love and meaning, and I cannot apologetically bury that fact. Therefore, I have chosen to describe sexual milestones and interactions that I believe are relevant. These were erotic events for me, and I would be delighted if I have described them well enough for my reader to be so moved when reading about them.

Love is, of course, much more than just sex, but the tingle that blends desire with lust serves only the cause of romantic love. Sexless men are not driven by sexual desire, and the special love that emerges when sexual intimacy is part of the equation is materially different from other types of love. It is the path I took to addressing the needs of this "romantic" love that I describe in this book. Romantic love is perhaps not as important in the grand scheme of things as other kinds of love: of God, parents, nature, children, or knowledge. But this is one focus of this book, and with the longing for fulfillment in romantic love comes the unavoidable baggage of sex.

As a child growing up, I seduced servants, milkmen, and strangers. I did not know enough about sex to know that such behavior may be considered "bad," or even that it was "sex." Little did I know that my spontaneous and seemingly natural drive was not considered "normal." None of my partners told me or complained about what we were doing together. As a result, I never felt any guilt or shame, nor did I feel that I had participated in anything at all unnatural. It was only much later in North America, in a Christian culture where sex is considered generically sinful, that I conceptualized these experiences as indicating that I was a special kind of person, one who required a gay identity.

Alas, I must hasten to add that Pakistan today has changed a great deal since my childhood. During the early 1990s, when I last visited, there was a climate of fear, violence, and immorality born of a new type of greed and corruption, based in materialism and blatantly self-serving appeals to "Islamic" values for political gain. Now I see less of the simplicity of my boyhood in Karachi. The middle class has emerged helter-skelter, complete with crass material values borrowed wholesale from the West. Perhaps they have always lurked just beneath the surface, and have now been released by the increase in travel abroad, and the redistribution of wealth through the export of labor to oil-rich mideast states. Exposure to Western-style individualism, along with increased trade and economic growth over the past decade, has also created a commercial veneer. This is good news for the Western visitor, though tourism is still an underdeveloped industry. Consumer goods are plentiful, and the monetary economy is well developed. Yet basic Pakistani values of loyalty, generosity, and welcoming hospitality still continue to flourish; they can be best experienced in the relatively peaceful and prosperous cities of the North, in the countryside, and in individual interactions. The residents of Karachi are still Pakistanis, but their lives are framed by the economics and dynamics of a barely functioning metropolis.

This book is a composite of fiction, fact, and fantasy. Identifying details of all characters, including the narrator's, have been significantly altered, and all locations have been changed. Some incidents, though real, are based on those of other Pakistani gay men.

This book cannot be used to draw any generalized conclusions about life in Pakistan. However, I grew up as a Pakistani Muslim and, as such, my experiences and observations are relevant to an understanding of life in Pakistan. None of the incidents described are materially false.

I owe a debt of gratitude to Dr. Stephen Murray for his long-distance encouragement to take the very difficult step of writing about my roots, my history, and my experiences. I first met Dr. Murray in Toronto during the heady 1970s era of gay liberation, and have followed his rise to become an eminent academician and scholar of homosexuality in cross-cultural perspectives. He is a prolific author who has laid the academic foundation for understanding same-sex issues. His array of books on related subjects span cultural boundaries and comprise an extraordinary collection.. His quiet persuasion, his ongoing guidance and advice, and his patient comments and encouragement, have provided the impetus necessary to complete this book (as well as my earlier writings, which have been well received and reprinted a number of times, including in languages other than English). Giving birth to a complete piece of writing often requires a skillful midwife, and this is one of Dr. Murray's virtues. Even more amazing has been our ability to work together efficiently by taming cyberspace to the task at hand. E-mail has become as indispensable as phone and fax, perhaps more so. It was also a pleasure for me to have become better acquainted with Dr. Murray's partner, Dr. Keelung Hong, and to appreciate his pithy wisdom and tolerant patience.

Special thanks are due to Eric Allyn, who managed an even longer distance relationship with diligence and exquisite finesse.

His tactful suggestions served to keep me focused, and his insight and feedback helped to me stay the course.

This book could not have been completed without the silent support and patience of my partner, Dick. Thank you, Dick, for understanding why I sometimes woke up in the middle of the night and crept off to my home office to work on the manuscript. Perhaps you alone come as close as anyone to understanding why I had to write this book, why I needed to release this burden of memory and experience from the silence of my soul, South Asian hyperbole notwithstanding. Your support and encouragement made it possible to actually do the work and not give up. This book is ultimately a serenade to our love, and my commitment to making the future work for us.

 # My Early Days

Discovery

The sweet aroma of *raat ki raani*[1] wafted into the area where we stood. Tiny, fragrant white blossoms dotted the dense brown bush, which flowered only on warm summer nights. This bush, one of several, was just by the gate, an eight-foot high metal door that was securely latched, and could be opened only from the inside with several moment's toil. The painted-over, but nonetheless, rusted latch did not fit well and squeaked its plaintive resistance. The gate could swing open about twelve feet to allow cars into the wide cemented driveway, canopied with grape vines. These vines were a particularly hardy variety, the grapes large and luscious, hanging in pendulous bunches. Often unpicked, they simply dropped to the

---

[1] This translates literally to "queen of the night." This flowering bush bears small white flowers that open only at night, and is popular for its sweet night-time fragrance.

cemented driveway. Occasionally, grapes nibbled by feral sparrows and crows would dribble their juices onto the parked cars below, and the drivers were constantly busy during this summer season scrubbing away grape juice from the dull, scratched, Karachi-tempered finish of the cars parked below.

Wazir and I were off to the side of this cemented driveway, standing on soft earth at the edge of the lawn. The gate was closed and locked, and the festooned light atop the concrete abutment to each side of the gate cut swaths on the side of the driveway. A high concrete wall topped with metal spikes enclosed the compound. We could see each other's faces clearly in the dusky and diffused haze of reflected light. I could smell the *naswar*[1] tobacco on his breath, and the light scent of the Lifebuoy soap he had bathed with. And I admired his sharp Pathan features.

The familiar sounds of the night from the other side of the wall were muted: the periodic ringing bells of passing bicyclists, loud neighborhood conversations, the soft purr of automobiles, or the *rat-a-tat* noise of motor-rickshaws as they drove by on what was already becoming an important thoroughfare in this remote part of the city.

Wazir had been with us as a *chowkidar*[2] for about a year. His reference was the previous *chowkidar*, who had been with us since his uncle, the *chowkidar* before him, had decided to go back home to the North, weary and old at forty-five. Wazir was perhaps twenty-one and spent his days gardening. His main job was to intercept and announce visitors to the household servants,

---

[1] This strong snuff-tobacco is popular among northern tribes. A wad is stuffed between the molars and the jaw, and nicotine is absorbed directly into the blood through the mucous membrane of the mouth.

[2] Gatekeeper.

or to take messages and turn away any who knocked on the front door without clear reason. At night he slept in a cot on the driveway. In the cool of the night, he had little to do but to sleep.

Wazir wanted to call it a night, but I insisted we play a little game. I was going to teach him English.

"Very important," I told him gravely, "to learn English. English is essential to advance in life these days."

How to start? I plucked a branch from a low hanging bougainvillea bush nearby.

"I will close my eyes," I told him, "and twirl this branch. Whichever part of your body it touches, I will say in English, and you then repeat it after me, and memorize it."

We stood under the full gaze of the lamplight as the game started and before he had gauged my intentions. With seeming innocence, I twirled the branch and let it brush against his body ostensibly by chance, naming his nose, his arms, and his stomach. As I moved the stick down, his eyes told me that he had connected the dots of my trajectory and guessed my intentions. Almost imperceptibly, we moved away from the light. This was getting interesting!

He was dressed in *shalwar-kameez*,[1] the traditional dress of men. The sober, dark gray *kameez* hung loosely down to his knees, covering his bunched up *shalwar*. The stick gently swung towards the loose fold between his legs. When I felt the time had come to forge forward to consolidate gains, I discarded it. As I expected, he wore no underwear.

---

[1] This loose clothing is popular in the hot and dusty climate of Karachi. Today, an equal number of locals wear Western-style shirts and trousers.

"And what is this in English?" I asked in Urdu[1] in my best pedantic style, while my hands pressed on his crotch to assess the bulge. His penis hung heavy and low in semitumescence between his legs. I stroked it lightly, to make sure my agenda was unambiguous. Wazir caught his breath and looked at me with horny tension. He glanced around furtively, anxiously. Investigating boldly, I drew out his nesting organ from within the cloth folds that had cocooned it between his legs. I cupped its heaviness in my palm, stroking it to erection through the thin layers of *shalwar* cloth. He parted his legs a bit, giving my hand access to caress his testicles.

"They are there," he whispered, having taken my investigation as a query into the completeness of his manhood. Perhaps he was taken aback by my desire to caress him further. Keeping up my pedagogic pretenses, I replied, "*In ka naam hai* 'balls'" ["These are called balls"], while gently kneading them.

I reached in through the side of his *kameez*, just at the slit, grasped his stiff pole, and continued to stroke it. There was now just one layer of cloth between us, the *shalwar*. The cloth was a light *mulmul* cotton, just a bit heavier than muslin, and I could feel his flesh hot in my hands. As I stroked, he leaned in relaxed pleasure against the side of the wall. His breath was coming in longer, more measured draws, and I was happy just to be with him, with this man, with this new intimacy that had flowered between us. He may have consented to the "game" initially to humor me, but his pleasure now was real.

I felt the drawstring of his *shalwar*, and tugged at it.

---

[1] The common language in Karachi. This language has much in common with Hindi, the common language in India. With variations, "street" versions of Urdu and Hindi can be understood throughout much of the Indian subcontinent.

"No, no," he protested. "Someone might come!"

The contest between his mind and his erect *lund*[1] was palpable. He looked around furtively, then raised and tucked the nape of his *kameez* under his chin and loosened his *shalwar*. I slid my hand down his smooth, hard belly, across his shaven pubes,[2] and closed it over his hard cock in a firm grasp. He exhaled sharply as I slowly stroked him.

"It is not very thick," he said, self-deprecatingly.

Indeed, it was a nice fit in my hand, well shaped and ample, long and slender. Its bulbous head grew harder when stroked with my firm grip. I could feel his slim body tighten and his groin arch forward, as his mouth gulped air. In the warm night breeze, I saw his wispy mustache hair blow in the wind and the glisten of a light sweat on his nose. He looked dazed and lifeless, his head slightly tilted and his perfect teeth mirroring the light, his eyes empty, his entire being caught up in simple rapture. I was in control of his feeling, and even of his breathing. I could inhale and exhale for him with one slow stroke of his shaft, or one light pinch to his balls. Like the responsive gearshift of sports car, by holding his penis, I held the basis of his being, for the moment, in my hand. His pleasure was simple and unblemished, and time was measured only in the quanta of stamina and stimulus, for my delight in this game was tempered by my ignorance of what to do next.

I played with him for several minutes. But this game was one-way. I was exploring his body, not inviting him to explore

---

[1] Penis.

[2] In Muslim custom, men shave their pubic area and underarms. This fosters hygiene. Since the anus is also washed with water after defecation, this generally means that the body's "sexual zones" are continuously clean and hence naturally aromatic.

mine. As a servant, he dared not take the initiative. I was strangely excited, and Wazir's erection was clearly central to this excitement. What was the next step? I did not know what to do, and he did not have the audacity to show me.

After some time at this game, we were both getting somewhat tired. I was clearly not ready to do much more, and he was ready for bed. I looked at my watch, and he mentioned that perhaps we should stop. I agreed, and quietly went inside the house and to bed, flushed and strangely tired.

ಅ ಬ

There was no change in the relationship between Wazir and me because of that interchange, and, indeed, no recognition or apparent memory of it in our further interactions. He was a servant in the household. I was one of the family he served. We had had a private moment together. Neither he nor I expected it to alter our relationship.

I would have gone back to see him again for another lesson, but a few weeks later he left to go back north to Swat[1] . to marry. His family had made wedding arrangements with a local girl he had never before met. Wazir had saved enough of his salary in our employment to be able to stay home in the North West Frontier province, and so did not return to Karachi.

I was thirteen years old at the time of this incident with Wazir. This was one of several sexual dramas of my pre-adolescence that I seem to have cunningly staged. In my ignorance, I could not choreograph and sustain them to successful climax, however. All my partners in these vignettes were of a lower status: servants, deliverymen, workers. None had the

---

[1] Swat is a province in Northern Pakistan. Once locally managed by a *Wali* or tribal leader, it was absorbed under the central Pakistan government shortly after the creation of Pakistan.

courage to help advance my progress along the road to sexual knowledge on which I wished to travel. With sensitivity and warmth, they tolerated my arousing them, playing with the markers of their manhood as though they were my toys, then imperiously dismissing them when I reached the limits of my imagination not yet catalyzed by hormones.

How did Wazir relieve himself after I had walked away, I now wonder? Could he have simply gone to bed, or did he masturbate himself and fertilize the *khad*[1] under the *raat ki raani* before sleeping that night?

The men I explored were in their sexual prime and functionally single, though some may have had wives and children somewhere in the background. Their erections were quick and solid. Their bodies were lean and tight, but I had not yet cultivated the good taste born of experience to worship them at the altar of eroticism. All good-humoredly consented to these games; none made me feel I was doing anything that was wrong, unnatural, or incomplete. My hand was clearly not the first that had touched them between their legs, as there was no expression of surprise or novelty. When we made contact, there was a tacit understanding that this had to be a private activity. They accepted pleasure as the opportunity arose and to the extent mutually agreeable but, with the customary gentleness of Pakistani men, they were able to limit this to sexual play, without stirring up aggressive demands for levels of sexual interaction that I was not ready for.

In the course of this early investigation of men's bodies, more specifically their genitals, I learned at a detached distance some things about the interaction between men, about the meaning of erections, and about the dynamics of pleasure. It was

---

[1] Manure.

only much later that I would understand that I, too, could participate in these experiences, and that such male pleasure was my birthright as well.

My sexual desires had unerringly found a home, unambiguous as iron filings in the face of a magnet. I would further explore this curiosity as an adolescent, but it would be only after several years of study and work abroad that I would return to truly experience the sexuality most Pakistani men take for granted. Without explanation or guilt, I knew from these early experiences that I preferred men.

To this day, I remember the look of pleasure and natural warmth in Wazir's eyes, once he had understood that his job was not in jeopardy, and that my interest in him was purely animal.

Karachi, The City

According to an old joke, Alexander the Great reached this sleepy fishing village near the mouth of the Indus river and, when he reached the Arabian Sea, thought he had discovered a freshwater lake. He knelt down to taste the water and spat it out, distastefully exclaiming *Khara-chee!*[1] and hence the name "Karachi" was born. This epithet characterizes the lack of affection most residents feel for this large and poorly planned commercial and industrial urban sprawl that today generates over seventy percent of the nation's gross national product.

Karachi is not an overtly sensual city. The streets are dusty and smoke-filled, with little organization and even less concern for civic niceties. There are no functional environmental or pol-

---

[1] *Khara* means "salty" in Urdu as well as in Sindhi, the predominant language.

lution controls, and the maze of streets connecting neighborhoods has developed in an *ad hoc*, unplanned way. Public transportation is inefficient and exhausting.

These are the predominant street images, glimpsed through a haze of gray and blue smoke: unmuffled motorcycles, rickshaws and large lorries that belch smoke, gaudily painted buses that race down clogged thoroughfares with men clinging to the sides. The air is poisonous, the water must be boiled before drinking, and twelve million people swarm the streets. Through it all, this amazing city continues to somehow function as it grows, swelled still more by immigrants from other parts of the country.

The stench of dung and urine blend with the smoky air, and pools of standing water on side streets and beside walls are fertile breeding grounds for flies and mosquitoes. Rounding a corner, one is likely to spot a squatter facing a wall in the process of urinating or defecating. This is a frequent sight, with its own etiquette. It is considered impolite to look at someone relieving himself in public. It is certainly impolite to edge sideways to get a look at his genitals! Gaudily dressed women from "Good Families" are driven by, or walk by with their *dupattas*[1] held against their noses. They soon disappear into compounds behind high walls, the only quiet refuge away from the public mess.

Amidst this filth and the swell of noise are food stalls and open-air restaurants that have music blaring from low-quality sound systems. Rich and alluring aromas of *gol guppas*, *jalebis*, and *aloo cholas* invade the senses, as people snack by the roadways and the crowd mills by. The rich aroma of food and enticing *filmi* music are constant temptations along any street. To the side,

---

[1] A gauzy shawl worn by women to cover their heads, or draped on the shoulders to cover exposed skin or hide the contours of the body.

the *paan wala*[1] hawks his wares, and the dark spittle squirted by *paan*-chewers paints the dirt. Dogs and cats scavenge what is thrown away.

Through this clutter and apparent confusion, the business of the day gets done on its own time scale. Errands become complex missions, and acquire dynamic identities of their own, as they merge with other goals, social and business. Most professional relationships are indeed personal, and friends are not a social nicety, but a necessity. There is a heavily structured social pecking order that keeps each transaction within its context, whether business or personal. This structure also permits a great deal of personal freedom—within well-defined and commonly understood, unspoken bounds. Whereas in the West, and particularly in the United States, the slightest hint of limits to freedom provokes an instant dash towards the perimeter to test constraints, in Pakistani society these bounds provide a great deal of personal security and liberty. Even the unconscionable disparity between the rich and poor provides the basis for charity, and a short instant path to connecting with humanity in its most basic form. Karachi is a study in survival, even for the rich. There are no illusions here. No amount of conceptualizing can dismiss the readily apparent despair of a starving beggar seeking alms from a *sahib*[2] stepping out of a Mercedes. At the same time, the needy so outnumber the privileged that the surrender of

---

[1] *Paan* is commonly eaten, after dinner or during the day. It is assembled by packing various ingredients in a *paan* leaf. These may include chopped *supari* (betel nut), *saunf* (anise seed), *naswar* (tobacco), shredded coconut, etc. Assembling a *paan* can be a major ritual in some households, and the *paan-daan* contains the individual ingredients that are mixed to assemble the *paan*.

[2] *Sahib* is a term of respect for a man, such as "sir." His wife would be referred to as *begum sahib*.

these privileges would have little real impact. The ethics of survival are raw and distasteful and without easy solutions.

There is little that is egalitarian about Pakistani society. Every individual interaction carries with it, to varying degrees, the baggage of family, economic status, ethnic background, and social position.

The social system is laced with seeming contradictions in convention. However, these inconsistencies blend to determine the basis for individual perception of what is natural and what is regarded as calculated sophistry. Individuals are generally warm-hearted, sincere, and forthright. Traditions of honor and community run deep in this very conservative country, and immigrants to Karachi bear testament to this. However, the simplicity and direct intimacy of a country bumpkin coexists very naturally with the canniness and necessary calculation needed to survive in what is essentially a social Darwinian model in action.

As in all Muslim countries, there is personal modesty in dress and demeanor in public. There is high value placed on *sharafat*.[1] Loyalty to family, good manners, courtesy, and generosity are admired. Greed, ambition, and the pursuit of individual goals at the expense of family are considered distasteful. Within these normative bounds, a wide range of individual expression flourishes. While over ninety-seven percent of the population is at least nominally Muslim, Islam in Pakistan is a variant that reflects its particular local history, and its relationship to other regional religions and traditions.

Men dress to hide their good looks in public. The *shalwar-kameez* is frumpish and baggy. The *shalwar* is a type of pajama, except that the waist is very wide—six to nine feet in circumference. A drawstring is passed through the waist and knotted in

---

[1] A *shareef* person espouses virtuous social values. *Sharafat* is the noun.

the front, usually at navel level. When worn, the garment has vertical folds that run from waist to ankle, so that it looks somewhat like a pantaloon. It is usually made of light cotton, which is very comfortable in the hot weather. Air circulates freely within the garment, which is loose and does not restrict motion.

There is usually no underwear worn beneath, so that a man's genitals can hang freely, yet be modestly covered. The folds disguise the thickest penis, or can make the smooth lines of a perfect thigh or buttock look frustratingly ordinary. Only through careful observation and studied experience can an observer learn to gauge what lies beneath the cloth, based on the movement of the cloth as the man moves. This challenge may add to the erotic allure of a beautiful man for the connoisseur man-watcher, and lends mystery and uncertainty about the treasures hidden beneath the folds of the plainer looking man. The *kameez* is designed to hide whatever a *shalwar* may reveal. It hangs to the knees, both front and back, protecting both crotch and ass from direct view. The *kameez* can naturally flare several inches in the front, and so can hide the sway of a tumescent penis and even permit an erection to be discreetly covered.

The *shalwar-kameez* is also the dressy alternative to the *dhoti* (or *langoti* in Punjabi), which is often worn by workingmen. The *dhoti* is a simple piece of cloth wrapped around the waist and tucked in so that the knot and folds are in front, over the crotch area. It generally extends below the knees to the ankles. This garment is very functional. It can be elevated so that it hangs higher, simply by raising the cloth and tucking it in. This helps keep the cloth dry when walking through water. The *dhoti* can be conveniently raised when squatting down to defecate or urinate in a public place, so that the genitals are protected from a side view. It can even be tucked in like a diaper, for workingmen who are around machinery or on a job site. It is not uncommon to see skeletal figures with sun-blackened skin clad in dirty white *dhotis* clambering around a construction site. These workers are often without shirts and with only a makeshift turban wrapped around their heads to protect them from the blazing sun.

Karachi is a multicultural and multiethnic city, and Pakistanis blend the history of several complex and ancient cultures. The texture of life is deeply rooted in tradition, and visitors attest to the amazing optimism and open friendliness and warmth of Pakistanis. Karachi is Pakistan's most heterogeneous city, and the variety in dress, language, food, and physical appearance is extraordinary.

It seems impossible to generalize or simplify Karachi life, and yet this is what I must do in order to tell my story. Much later, I would return to Karachi to visit, and discover the template of the sexual city. This large metropolis houses many mysteries, and among them is the "Quiet World," the world that coexists with the noisy bustle of commercial middle-class morality in action.

Pakistanis love to talk, emote, express their views. We are generally outgoing, friendly, personable, and genuinely goodhearted people. Within social and economic constraints, men and women act freely and forthrightly. Their actions are simple, defensible, and communally supportable. There is little notion of personal privacy. Locking doors is unusual, except to protect property. People drop in to visit unannounced, so there is little that can be hidden. Since relationships are traced back to their origins, each new friend must be fit into a social framework before he or she can be properly introduced within the family. Social and family connections are immutable, a new entrant from a different social segment is an outsider who must be connected to the family through a firewall to permit managed familiarity. The pool of insiders must be restrained in their actions, since each interaction becomes part of the permanent communal record.

Because so much is visible, a great deal of personal eccentricity is tolerated and even accepted, in acknowledgment of inevitable human diversity. Differences are often simply ignored and overlooked. Deviance is treated with humanity, charity, and any anguish is kept private—ideals and standards to the contrary. The crotchety spinster who chatters endlessly about the unruly neighborhood boys; the eccentric old man who has a young boy massage his legs and thighs; the spry elderly man who dwells on the therapeutic value of honey enemas—these are all colorful variants that coexist contentedly above the surface and are accepted with good humor. Every family has skeletons in its closet, which is fine as long as they do not rattle. Skeletons are generally left in peace, ignored out of *lehaaz*.[1] There is an element of fatalism about circumstances that leads to an unexpected kind tolerance for deviance.

Within Karachi is the Quiet World, into which I wandered in my search for satisfaction. The Quiet World is the world of the unspoken and the unseen, in which privacy is honored. This does not mean that people do not speak when in this world. In fact, they natter endlessly. But this is privileged communication, not to be disclosed to the bourgeois mainstream. This is the world in which the *shareef* do not wander. It is the world of prostitutes and their customers, illicit music and dance, romance and poetry, unsanctioned lovemaking and brief encounters. It is a world that is rich with variety, an arena that is neither disclosed nor condoned, neither acknowledged nor respected. The unspo-

---

[1] Consideration for others.

ken secrets of a society speak volumes about its cultural values. In Pakistan, where family honor and integrity are paramount, what is Quiet is that which has the potential to harm the family, and this is relegated to the Quiet World.

In this Quiet World, sexual contact follows human desires, not social norms. In my return visit to the city after some years in North America, I found that it teemed with a rich and varied range of prospective sexual partners. The equation is simple: wherever there are men, there is the potential for sexual contact. The streets, the parks, the beaches teem with young men, many single and away from home and the requirements of conformity. Often their extended family is rooted in the villages outside Karachi, or frequently up north.[1] Many live with parents; others, with roommates or in makeshift housing provided by an employer. These men all need to be serviced sexually and, since marriage is a sign of stable maturity many have yet to attain, they have no one but themselves, or each other, with whom to seek sexual release. Since the militant heterosexualist norm of the West is largely absent, there is a need, and occasionally the opportunity, to wander into the Quiet World for a little relief.

The key limiting factor that constrains sex between consenting men is the lack of privacy. As a result, where lonely equals are concerned, sex must become, of necessity, a public event. In the late hours of the night, I have seen two men asleep with each other on a small cot in public, near a construction site, a blanket covering their bodies, passersby honoring their need for

---

[1] Karachi is the engine of much of the job growth in Pakistan. As such, it is a magnet for men seeking employment. These men are from the northern provinces of the Punjab, the NWFP (North Western Frontier Province), or from Gilgit, Hunza, and other remote areas.

privacy. Were they just sleeping, or were they having sex? It mattered not. There is similarly no record, other than anecdotal, of the frequency and pervasiveness of sex between men in college dormitories, schools, and other similar institutions, but it is probably substantial. Perhaps the only truly democratic contacts in Pakistan are the silent sexual contacts between men in public places. They span class, status, ethnic background, and convention; men vote as individuals to decide with whom they will share intimacy, and all social customs fade into the background when faced with the primacy of the sexual dance.

For the workingman with some discretionary income, *malishees*[1] can provide a late-night massage and, in the dark, sex under the stars for a bit more. *Hijras*[2] and male prostitutes can be bought and have private space, but they are more expensive. Female prostitutes are much more expensive.

The city is an open-air "meat market," best inspected while driving. Within this giant crucible of cruising, the street corner and bus stop are places to stand and, with the right bearing and glance, a pickup is usually fairly easy. The seasoned purveyor of the flesh trade usually distinguishes himself in the crowd with ease. Equally likely, a young man will expect some money. However, most single men, whether at street corners or in parks, if they are alone, can be sweet-talked into the type of camaraderie that leads to sexual contact. Typically, the sex is anal, with the younger man the receptor. When money is involved, however, other arrangements may be negotiated, including oral sex.

Are these straight, lonely men without women, or are they "gay"? This question has relevance only when asked in the

---

[1] *Maalishee* is a masseur.
[2] Transvestites, sometimes *castrati*.

West. For the participants themselves, what happens between two people depends entirely upon the chemistry, the mood, time and money needs, and the availability of privacy. These contacts may be perfunctory and anonymous, or connected in a regular relationship that continues over time. Either one or both men may be married. Neither man would expect such a Quiet relationship to blossom into anything more, irrespective of how much romance creeps into it. Under no circumstances could their sexual partners be even considered for integration into family life, let alone could a male-male relationship become an alternative to the family.

My Childhood and Family

My father was a mid-level bureaucrat in the Pakistan government and, as such, we led a privileged life of relative affluence. Our house was initially in the Clifton area, and we later moved to the Defense Housing Society. Both of these houses were large and had splendid gardens, thanks to the largesse of the government, which also supplied a retinue of servants. We had a constant stream of official visitors, and my father was always involved in important matters of state. A gravity and sense of serious purpose pervaded the household. The country was young, and there were issues to work out that required active leadership. As one of the support staff, my father would be called upon to participate in meetings, host dignitaries, and attend social functions. Therefore, he did not have much time left over to spend with his children. Since my siblings were generally healthy and happy, they could be summoned when needed, so that he could delight in their company.

I was the odd child out; my childhood was unusual and atypical of Pakistani children.

I was a sickly child and not expected to survive beyond infancy. I had a case of infantile eczema, which started when I was less than six weeks old. This now-treatable skin disease reduced me to a scratched-up, swollen pulp. Doctors had to tie my hands to keep me from scratching myself to death. The prescription of the day was coal-tar, a smelly preparation that derived from the same material used to lay roads and roofs. It has the consistency of molasses and an unpleasant, pungent odor. It was applied all over my tiny body, to help soothe the scratching and itching. After application, the coal-tar was lightly bandaged over, so that I was covered and trussed like an Egyptian mummy for much of the time. To this day, my skin is the weak link, and when stressed I break out in a (relatively mild) case of eczema. Once every few years, it gets bad enough that I need to go in for an intramuscular shot of hydrocortisone in my buttocks. This instantly clears it up. Cortisone, the miracle drug, had not been invented when I was an infant or was, at least, unavailable in Pakistan.

I was the fourth child of six. Five of the six children were born over a period of just eight years; my eldest brother was born five years before the pack. When my father decided it was finally time to raise a family, he went to work in earnest! For a long time, then, the house was occupied by five screaming and demanding young children and infants—this along with friends and relatives who sometimes came in to socialize and sometimes stayed with us, Pakistani style. Since our family was originally from Lahore, in the Punjab, we had very few close relatives in Karachi who could be counted on for much help. A generation earlier, many had migrated to what was now India, and lived in Bombay. Crossing the border to visit Pakistan was a practical impossibility, since India and Pakistan were continually in a state of belligerency. For practical purposes, therefore, we functioned as a relatively small family unit by Pakistani standards, though perhaps not as compact and isolated as a Western-style nuclear family.

Since it was not possible for my mother to effectively take care of six children simultaneously, the most problematic one (me) was turned over for rearing to my grandmother—my mother's mother—shortly after birth. The timing was good, since my mother had just lost her father in an automobile accident, which had left my grandmother quite distraught with grief. For all practical purposes, she was already living with us. Her children were grown, and she did not want to live alone. This seemed like a good way to refocus her attention, and also to give me the special care that I needed. She quickly adopted me as her own, and lavished her full attention on me. This also allowed me to stay at home and be absent from school for extended periods of time, on grounds of ill health. I found that I enjoyed staying at home and did not miss the competitive and worldly life that school promised. I also learned to appreciate reading and, as a convalescing invalid, I found the passing days to be quite agreeable.

My health did not improve as I left infancy behind. I developed chronic bronchitis, which, along with a host of other ailments, kept me home and away from regular schooling and the social company of other boys. In reading I found solace for the sadness caused by my isolation and great despair in my lack of routine connection with the rest of the family. My daily experiences differed from those of others in the family. They would leave in the morning; I would stay at home. They would experience the outside world and return in the evening, whereas I would have spent the day at home, reading or sick in bed.

Since I was a son—the second one of three, and the sickly one—my father would try from time to time to connect with me. My older brother was by nature distant, reserved and unaffectionate, and almost constantly away with friends. He had left to join a boarding school in Murree at the age of twelve and eventually entered the army at age sixteen. We rarely saw him, except during short visits. My father's overtures to me were generally jocular and unsympathetic and, typically, my grandmother would possessively intercede on my behalf, explaining my latest ailment for his benefit. He found her intervention annoying and her presence irritating. Their relationship was tense. He wanted me to be available for him on his terms, while she insisted that he pay consistent attention to me. Her insistence would contribute to his further stubborn withdrawal. Since I was the battleground for this conflict between them, I bore the brunt of his retaliation and her overprotection. This rivalry and underlying tension around me added to the unpleasantness of a sick childhood.

My earliest memories are those of the rest of the family going off on a Sunday to the beach at Clifton, leaving me alone at home, sick in bed, with only my grandmother to keep me company. While she was all mine, she alone did not suffice to replace the rest of my family. She was a brilliant woman who encouraged me to be optimistic about the future, and taught me to develop and maintain high standards. I owe her a debt of gratitude. However, try as she might, she could not replace my parents.

During this period I was sickly, plump, underexercised, and overfed. My grandmother, a practitioner of herbal medicine, believed that proper nutrition was essential to health and that my father did not pay enough attention to me. My father believed that my ailments were largely psychosomatic, the result of my grandmother's overattentiveness and overindulgence. Both were probably right. Their rivalry in the matter was exacerbated by my mother's unwillingness to take sides or, more specifically, my side. She was devoted to my father, yet close to her mother, and the issue of how to handle me caused strain and much discussion. Occasionally the undercurrent of tension spilled over into open argument, and my mother's role would be to placate the warring parties, without asserting her opinion in any forceful way.

My father had very little willpower regarding food and sweets and, as a result, was constantly battling a weight problem. He did not follow his own prescriptions of moderation and self-control. This seemed to make him more determined than I did. My grandmother, on the other hand, felt that as a child I needed to eat my fill and constantly subverted my father's instructions. Food was, therefore, an important battleground for the debate between my father and grandmother.

The dinner table arrangement reflected the family tree. The oval-shaped table had its head facing the kitchen door from whence the food emerged. There was one chair at its head, with four chairs to each side. The foot of the table had one or more chairs, depending on who would be joining us for the meal. My father sat at the head of the table, a tall floor lamp at his left casting a bright light over his place setting. Often he would read a magazine, against my mother's objections. Even when he wasn't reading, he made little conversation during meals. I sat to his immediate left. Flanking me was my grandmother, and to my brother's right was my mother. To her right was my younger brother, followed by my youngest sister and my other sisters. My oldest sister typically seated herself at the foot of the table, but the dynamics that concerned me were at the upper end of the table, near its head.

Unlike me, my youngest brother grew up skinny. Therein lay the seeds of our dinnertime circus. My mother would often literally spoon-feed her youngest son, her favorite. He would refuse, she would persist. He would whine that he wasn't hungry, she would warn of dire consequences—starvation or worse. Across the table from him I would eat silently, consuming what was on my plate. From time to time my grandmother would pile additional food on my plate in silence, and I would clear it again. My father meanwhile would be struggling with his diet, and would instruct me to control my portions, to reduce my weight. My grandmother would differ with him from time to time. My mother and siblings ate in quiet tension during these altercations.

Aside from the preoccupation with food, the other focus was to do something significant enough to merit attention from my father. We were expected to do well in school. Not just well: we were expected to come first in our classes, and this was the only way to win recognition from him. Conversely, to slip in school was to incur the clear, but very subtle, put-down by my father.

Mother: "Look, Farzana [my older sister] came first in her class!"

Father: "Very good! [said with the hint of a slight smile, clearly pleased. Turning to me, he said:] "How did you do?"

Me: "I came fifth in my class"

Father: "Who came first?"

Me: "Shahid." [Shahid was a tailor's son, who had been admitted to the school on scholarship.]

Father: "You were beaten by the tailor's son! Perhaps you will end up becoming a tailor."

Then, he turned back to reading the newspaper. He would not stand for second best.

My youngest brother, though an average student, was slim, which raised him in my father's esteem. Also, he was healthy, and could participate in all the activities and outings. Hence, the seeds of rivalry for my father's acceptance were sown between my youngest brother and me. By overtly favoring him with affection and attention, my father could, in one fell swoop, strike against my grandmother's role, express his admiration for my brother's ability to control his weight (through a metabolic quirk, no particular effort of his own), and express his need to be affectionate with his son. What got squashed in this family drama were my feelings.

The normal male child learns about the world through rough-and-tumble experience, through jumping in and messing it up, through sport and play, and through dynamic experimentation with relationships. My childhood, conversely, was distant and academic. I saw much of life through windows, observed it played out by others. At school, I was excused from physical training and sports activities, so that I watched other boys at play, from a distance. I was accustomed to sitting on the sidelines—different, excluded, separate. I had to invent my world through observation and imaginative construction, not through direct experience and interaction. I must have been quite a lonely child, awkward and detached. It was, however, the only life I knew.

My life seemed artificial to me; acting rather than living. Others revealed themselves truthfully through action and emotion: their lives were testimonies to their worries and goals, their passions and pleasures. Their possession of the world was natural; they had no need for self-awareness. I, on the other hand, felt that my life was hidden and my feelings were forever secret. My role was to mimic and pass, to learn roles with belief and conviction. I would be an actor on a stage where the other players were living ordinary lives. How I envied their unconcern about how they were perceived, their complete sense of belonging!

To construct my world, I had to conduct constant experiments, to collect data points with which I could fashion a picture of how people were supposed to function. To understand the methods of interpersonal interaction, I observed the roles people played. Like an artificial-intelligence machine, I absorbed thousands of scenarios and stimulus-response vignettes, decomposing, organizing, and preparing them for use. I felt as though I did not know what my genuine responses and passions were, or whether I had any. I just knew that when I reacted and how I reacted—surprise or anger or fear—they must appear genuine. So I carefully observed others. This early training came in quite useful when I left the country to come to North America. It took me very little time to adjust to the interpersonal system, or culture, and to decide what to mimic and internalize, and what to resist.

During my sequestered childhood, I regarded sex with the same pseudo-clinical detachment that I reserved for life overall.

Early Awakenings

Throughout my preteen years, I was often admitted to the Civil Hospital[1] in Karachi for extended stays, for various ailments. It became a second home. While the area outside the hospital was crowded and dirty, the hospital itself was an island of serenity. Since my father was employed as a government servant by the Central Pakistan Government, I had easy access to a private room.

The private rooms at Civil Hospital were large and airy. The ward I was placed in was constructed to be temporary, and consisted of an array of these rooms, with common walls, stacked barracks-style, like matchboxes. Each room opened to the covered verandah with cemented floors. The strident chatter of doctors and nurses, the yells of sweepers and personal attendants, and the acrid smell of liberally applied disinfectant frame my memories of this early period. In many ways it was like being in a war, since there were long periods of inaction punctuated with bursts of activity, and I could influence none of these. I was a passive occupant of this pleasant prison. I could not run in the halls, play with other children, or laugh with others, but then no one expected me to play like a normal child in that abnormal environment.

Except for occasional visits, I rarely saw my mother and father while I was in the hospital. My mother was busy with her other children and their demands, and my father was busy building a career. In the hospital even more than at home, my grandmother was, therefore, my major connection to the family. She was my constant attendant, and slept in the same room. She

---

[1] Civil Hospital is one of the major hospitals in Karachi. It is located in old Karachi, off Bunder Road, in a dense, congested neighborhood.

brought food to me, argued with the doctors and nurses to make sure I was properly attended to, and consoled me. I was isolated and protected, lonely, and introspective. My hospital stays would last several weeks at a time, after which I would return home, even more detached from the hubbub of family life than before.

When I was ten, I went in for a tonsillectomy. The procedure required general anesthesia, and standard practice required abstinence from food and drink for several hours prior to the surgical procedure. I was checked in a few days before surgery. The nurse primarily assigned to me was cheerful and friendly, so I was content, if a bit anxious.

She explained to me that an enema would be required on the day the surgery was to be done, to clear my intestines. This meant that warm water would be introduced into my colon, and after a few minutes I would go to the toilet and flush out my lower gastrointestinal tract. Operationally, this meant that I would lie in bed, turn to my side, pull my pants down to my knees, and permit a lubricated tube to be shoved up my anal cavity. The other side of this greased tube would be connected to a large bulb full of warm water. After the tube had gone in far enough, warm water would gush up my ass.

The time approached and the assembled group, including my grandmother, faded in the background. A ward boy was summoned in to do the deed. This was standard hospital procedure. Where male genital areas and associated body parts of men and boys were concerned, a ward boy did the work required. My nice nurse left me. This was now a male thing.

The ward boy approached. He was dark and good-looking, with a clipped mustache and clear Sindhi features. He looked bored but, as our eyes met, I felt his look.

I whimpered my refusal. No, I did not want this, I was too embarrassed. Everyone rushed back to my bedside.

"It will just take a moment," they assured. "There's no pain, so don't worry." I told my grandmother in no uncertain terms that I did not want the man to do the inserting, but rather the cheerful and pleasant nurse. Once they figured out what the problem was, the ward boy shrugged and left, and it was left to the nurse to complete the job. Everyone was amused. She turned me over, I lowered my pants, she shoved it in, and the warmth of the saline liquid invaded me. Moments later, I stumbled over to the toilet and let out a strong and steady stream of salt water and feces, then returned to my bed, squeaky-clean from the inside out.

In retrospect, there was clearly an erotic component to the enema, which I had preconsciously identified and related to the man who approached me. He was going to take a hard, phallic-shaped dildo tube and shove it up my bottom. I was not going to let him. I would resist, and this I did. Perhaps I thought he would hurt me, whereas nothing the nurse could do would have that effect. Perhaps I instinctively felt that it was his penis, his erection, the hard-on that the nurse was simply not equipped with, that would enter and violate me. Perhaps it was this that terrified me, and perhaps I feared even then my initiation into the world of the sexual, with men, the objects of my desire. Perhaps I surmised that my preference would be to insert my own erect penis and not to take those of others, though I had no direct knowledge of such things at twelve years of age.

Delicious Dalliances on the Home Front

Most of my childhood time alone was spent at home, and much of this time was free from responsibilities and chores. It was therefore natural for me to concern myself with the men around me. There were several male house servants who formed a stable core of the household help. They were almost "family," in the sense that any interchange with them could not be easily forgotten. They were therefore out-of-bounds for sexual experimentation. Fortunately, this proscription did not apply to outside servants such as the gardener and night watchman, or to the various handymen and other transient workers who were temporarily in the family's employ.

To fathom the world of sexual desire, I constructed experiments in the laboratory of my environment. Experiments require a certain clinical distance between observer and experimental object. I could not afford to be affected personally by these data, lest the experiment be tainted by feeling. The process was quite methodical: identify my targets, carefully arrange the circumstances, and then actually execute the experiment. In retrospect, my approach was perversely clinical. My goals were to understand the nature of sexual arousal and sexual desire, and the dynamics of the male sexual apparatus and its function. At the tender age of fourteen, I had yet to experience ejaculation. Even after wet dreams gushed forth their creamy excrescence, I did not know for a long time how to stimulate myself to orgasm. Lacking even this basic knowledge, but knowing that men and their penises fascinated me, I took an inductive, empirical approach.

In retrospect, I find it amusing that I went about my work so diligently and methodically. As with Wazir, I constructed situations in which I would get close to men with no one else around, then stimulate their genitals and build a space of sexual intimacy with them. This was probably not the way most boys my age received their early sexual instruction, but the approach served well to provide me with the knowledge I needed at that stage of my life in Pakistan. The class difference between my sexual objects and me served further to ensure my control of the experimental environment; were there not this difference, I may well have been "used" rather than the "user."

The Painter's Helper

It was time to paint the living room and dining room areas. A painter was hired, a large, older man with a bushy beard and a gruff, hard-bitten look. His young helper, though, captured my attention. He had smooth, wheat-colored skin, a deep sun-darkened face, chiseled good looks, and a lean, light body. When I first saw him laughing with one of the servants, his smile was clear, his teeth bright, and his aura magnetic. He was breathtaking.

The young man's work clothes consisted of a pair of loose shorts and a T-shirt. When he moved, I could see his genitals swaying. He had nothing on under those shorts! As I watched him, I felt his magnetism, and I would stand and watch him work in the main room. People walked through this room while the painting was in progress, and there was no real privacy, so I feigned interest in the process of painting. Days admiring this young painter passed.

I saw my chance when he next had to paint the bathroom. To reach the ceiling, he needed to climb a ladder, and to reach the high corners, I saw that he would lean over, and put one foot on the door-frame for support. This meant that his shorts would open up! My heart pounding, I stood under him to watch. Transfixed, I waited and maneuvered my position, and looked up.

His heavy testicles swayed visibly a few feet above me as he lurched to steady himself. Then, as he moved back and forth while applying paint, his penis came into view. It looked magnificent, a truly heavenly body from my earthbound vantage point. I was possessed by wonder and excitement. I watched transfixed, as long as I could, my face flushed.

He came down off the ladder, and, thinking his task was completed, I asked an innocuous question to keep him here.

"What color do you think is the best for a bedroom?"

As he talked with me and we moved around looking at whether various sections of the bathroom had indeed been properly painted, my hand "casually" touched his penis in passing. We continued. I touched it again, by accidental design. We continued our meaningless conversation, except that my hand was still pressed against his crotch, his dick was getting harder, and he began to breathe more deeply.

Seemingly in a flash, it was erect and naked on its own, freed from the wispy cloth that had cradled it. His penis was beautifully proportioned, hard and long and horizontal. He had not moved. I reached up and stroked it.

"Someone will come," he uneasily whispered and moved away. Facing away from me, he tucked his penis under his waistband, then climbed back to resume his painting. I waited.

When he was done, I asked him to come into my room to see if a paint job was required. After he entered my room, I locked the door and, when I turned back to him, his organ was out and ready without any help from me. It stood erect, inviting me to address its needs. I played with it, needing to feel it, wanting to caress it, yearning to consume it somehow. I fondled his testicles, marveled at their size and heft. His penis was like a thick salami protruding from his loins. It was smooth and velvety to the touch, hard and unyielding to the squeeze. Its large, acorn-shaped head was smooth and responsive to the lightest stroke. As I ran my hand over it, under it, around it, he shuddered as it arced in response. Then I used both hands to try to better encompass his beautiful *lund*. I felt a tenderness within me for this stranger, the only part of whom I knew with any certitude was his penis. With wonderment, I felt a deep and blissful awe and knew that this moment was important, that I'd never forget this sight or this feeling. This marvelous beast in my hand, this warm cucumber, this organic link connected me to myself, and had the power to persuade and to protect. He enjoyed my tender ministrations, then turned to leave as he concluded that I did not have any further plan of action.

I lured him back to my room from time to time, just to touch and play with his dick. A couple of times, he touched my ass.

"No," I said firmly.

"Please, can I just put my hand inside and touch?" he pleaded.

"No!" was my fearful and heartless response. He knew what he wanted, yet I was not ready to go that far.

Eventually, he tired of this game. Now recognizing me as a frustrating cock-tease, he started to refuse my invitations. One day, I found him in the back, painting the outside stairway that led to the roof. I reached out and grabbed him, made him hard.

"No," he said after a while. He continued painting. Playtime was over.

☙ ❧

When I later returned to Karachi as a seasoned adult, I held a penis that felt just like that of the painter's assistant. It happened one spring evening, at dusk. I was cruising the roundabouts. A handsome boy tracked my car with his eyes, obviously interested. I locked eyes with him. He beckoned, as though seeking a ride. I stopped, and he got in. He gave me a penetrating look, then a dazzling smile. His hand rested briefly on my knee, a halfway step marking its progress towards its destination. He smoothly reached over and stroked my penis through my trousers, then skillfully unzipped me. We had not said two words to each other.

I reached over and stroked his lean muscular leg, then under his *kameez* and into his warm center. I curled my fingers around his organ, moist with sweat at its confinement, lifted it clear of the pincer grip of his legs, and coaxed it to blossom. Its hardness filled my hand and pressed against my palm. As I moved my hand against the thick shaft, from stem to stern, from fore to aft, from base to proud firm head, with a corkscrew motion, feeling his belly tighten against my wrist, feeling his thighs open and his body slump lower in the car seat, I remembered my painter and his manhood that had been my plaything, little as I knew then how to use it. It had felt just like this in my hand. The same shape, the same robust kick when stroked. This time was different, though. Now I knew what this organ was designed for. Now I knew that this incredible organic machine was designed to be driven to an ultimate peak in passion.

I deftly loosened this young man's *shalwar* and freed his cock, erect against his belly, of its humid cloth confines. He was squirming under my fingers' caresses, as he turned sideways, bent over, and engulfed my erection in his mouth. What expertise! I drove blindly, letting the car slow to a snail's crawl. His mouth, warmer than any haven, tighter than any ass, continued its movements of heat and pressure, while my right hand was stroking his shaft. We were in a contorted embrace, a tangle of connections. I was gasping; he was squirming. I was stroking with focus and zeal. Through the fog of passion, I became vaguely aware that the traffic was starting to build, people appeared on the streets, and streetlights seemed to materialize.

I exploded into his mouth just as I felt his warm cum spurt all over my hands, dripping over his *shalwar*, drops snaking between his thighs, now clenched again. He kept his mouth on me, sucking me dry. Then he sat up and mumbled, "Stop." So I pulled over to the side of the road. He opened the door and spat my warm cum onto the road where it spattered on the pavement; it must have sizzled from our passion and the heat of his mouth. Then he reached down and scraped cum from his clothes using his fingers, and flicked it on the road several times, until it was obvious that the residue would be part of him for the evening, and would perfume him the rest of his journey.

"I have to go," he said. "That is fifty rupees please."

"Fifty rupees!" I gasped, "That is highway robbery!" (That was almost $2.00.)

"I think you live abroad," he commented matter-of-factly, "you can afford it and, besides, look, I'll have to get my clothes washed now."

"Okay," I said, and paid him that amount, plus a small tip. As he raised his body to leave, I ran my hand around his buttocks, and stroked his peach-shaped buns, then reached under his parted legs from behind, caressed his perineum, and lightly fingered his asshole. He stayed motionless, allowing me to play with him awhile. He looked over.

"Maybe next time," he whispered huskily. "How long are you here? I stand where you saw me, usually around this time."

Then he leapt from the car, I accelerated, and he disappeared. . . .

Tailored To Please

The tailor would come in daily. He was employed by my family to work on a project, which would take him several weeks to complete. During this time, he was provided with equipment and space in the house to work.

Every day, working diligently, he sat at the landing at the top of the stairway leading to the upper floors. He would operate the manual sewing machine with his legs, while sitting on a stool, his back against the wall and facing the stairwell. Around his sewing machine on the floor was a cloth on which lay his materials and work-in-progress.

The tailor's skin was charcoal black, and he had beady green eyes and elegant high cheekbones. He had the tight, skinny build of a workingman, and a trim mustache. He was quite fastidious about his personal grooming. He changed his clothes daily, most often a light and comfortable *shalwar-kameez*. He was always freshly shaved, and his hair was slicked down with gel. Like an artist creating clothes to fit a pattern in his mind, once he started working, he was dedicated to completing the job. He worked steadily and furiously, a look of concentration on his face.

The rooms around him were generally empty during the day. Someone coming up the steps to his little private space could be easily heard, providing ample warning.

I would sit next to him and watch him work. As far as he was concerned, I was just one of the pesky kids in the family. I asked him about his life and his family, his wife and child. His answers were brief, with no elaboration, and he seemed so inaccessible, yet he would occasionally flash a fleeting smile when there was something amusing to share. Unapproachable, yet alluring.

One day he came in wearing a *dhoti*. I remarked that he had changed his clothing, and he said, "Yes, the weather is warmer, and I prefer wearing the *dhoti* since it makes me feel cooler."

As he started to work, I sat next to him. I asked him how it was worn, and he explained that it was wrapped around the waist, and then he pointed to the knot covering his belly button.

"Really?" I feigned surprise, and reached out to feel the thick knot, where the two ends of the cloth are brought together. "Oh," I articulated my innocent train of thought, "so the two folds open in the front, is that right?" He continued working.

My hand was exploring the garment, and was already under his *kameez*. Boldly, I found the edge of cloth. Rummaging in his crotch, I found his sleeping organ, tightly held between his legs. I ran my fingers along the rough stubble on his pubes to its base, traced its circumference, and moved along its flaccid trail from base to head. My fingertip lingered near the head, gently inviting it to awaken. It lay quietly at first, and then I felt it stirring. He continued working furiously through all this.

Then, his legs parted involuntarily as if his erection had wedged them apart. His penis was hard, but lied flat at thigh level, on his lap, confined by his *dhoti*. I again reached under the cloth to directly contact his flesh and stroked it. He glanced towards the stairway, obviously uneasy that someone might stumble onto this scene. I continued to explore, feeling its shape. It was wide, thick, and short, and peaked into a narrow head. I was now stroking its full length, and his organ was no longer supine. It was now independently poised like a bird in flight.

"It is very hard," was my unnecessary comment.

"This goes into my wife once a week," was his reply.

"Really? How do you do it?"

"Well," he said, "I climb over her, my body between her legs, and I put it inside her."

"Really?" I continued to stroke his penis.

"Stop . . . the water will come out. Then my clothes will get soiled. Besides," he said sensibly, "I have work to do."

My mood was spoiled and, besides, it was lunch time, and I had to go. However, we had established a new beachhead of intimacy together.

The next day I went back to see my tailor when he had on his normal *shalwar-kameez*, and I now had no compunction about putting my hand to his crotch, stroking him erect, and playing with him while he worked. It amused me to see him try to concentrate while his erection throbbed in my hands.

One day, when the house was empty except for my tailor and me, and the servants were busy, I asked him to show me what he meant by "the water coming out."

"No," he said, "Don't bother me." His manner was brusque, but not definitively final.

I persisted. We went to the bathroom and I locked the door. I loosened his *nara*,[1] and his *shalwar* fell to the ground. For the first time, I was with a naked and willing man in private. I felt strangely intimate, deeply excited, and breathless with anticipation. I stroked his black dick. It was larger than I had imagined, now that he was standing. He told me to continue stroking and made small sounds of pleasure. I did not stop as his body tightened, and he grasped the washbasin firmly, one hand on each side. He seemed lost in concentration. Then I saw what he

---

[1] The drawstring used to hold the *shalwar* in place.

meant by the "water" coming out. White cream spewed forth and, when I stopped stroking it, his fist took over. Gradually the initial spurts diminished to a trickle. I had witnessed my first ejaculation! I marveled at it, and at his satisfied look. He had unlocked the puzzle that had tormented me. Through simple example, he had shown me what this was all about. Later I was to practice this with others.

The Wayward Pathan

Later that year, we hired a houseboy. He was the relative of one of our servants, and his job was light cleaning and dusting, odd jobs and errands, and helping the other servants. He was a Pathan, and young—I guessed he was perhaps seventeen. I could see by the peach fuzz on his upper lips that he had passed puberty. His playful eyes and relaxed demeanor made me realize that he was a good candidate for me, and that his interests could be broadened.

One day, he was cleaning my room, and I asked him where he was from.

"Near Abbotabad.[1] My family's village is within a bus ride."

I asked him how old he was and whether he had been to school. He answered that he was not sure how old he was, but perhaps in his twenties.[2] I laughed and commented that at that age he was becoming a man. He modestly agreed that yes, he was. Then I asked whether he had hair on his body and he proudly confirmed that yes, he did.

"Show me," I said. He had fallen neatly into my trap.

"Somebody may come in," he muttered nervously.

---

[1] A town in Northern Pakistan.
[2] Age is not always well tracked among rural villagers.

"Don't worry," I said and locked the door. He opened his shirt so that I could see the wisps of hair on his chest. Then, he raised his *shalwar* to show me his legs, smooth and muscular, with wisps of down turning dark. I ran my finger over the wispy hair above his upper lip, and commented that he was growing a mustache. He grinned proudly. I raised his *kameez* to inspect the hair that was curling around his belly button. I then pointed to his crotch and boldly asked, "How about there?"

He laughed nervously. "No, I can't show you down there."

"Come on!" I urged lightly. "I want to see."

After some hesitation, he loosened his *shalwar* and lowered it just enough for me to see his shaved pubes.[1] The stubble was soft to my exploring touch. Then my hand touched the base of his penis, and laughing with delight, I reached in and extracted it.

"No!" he said half-heartedly protested, but I was already playing with it, and it was already hard.

As I fondled his erection, I could sense his wonderment at the sensations this caused. He was just becoming an adult, and this was clearly not something he had had much opportunity to experiment with, living in close quarters with his relatives.

"Come to the bathroom," I said, "let us see what happens."

I positioned him against the sink, then continued to stroke him. His body arched and swayed, and his face was focused with a remarkable intensity. While I was experimenting with his body, he was clearly finding out more about himself.

"Stop! Stop!" he suddenly cried, then cupped his hand in front of his bursting dick as though to stem the flow of a torrent he sensed was on the way. But I didn't stop. Suddenly, to

---

[1] By showing me what was in effect his lower belly, he was in a gray zone and had not yet violated any clear principle of immodesty.

his surprise and my satisfaction, he squirted an immense load of semen that must have shot at least five feet. It squirted against the wall, on the mirror, on the washbasin, on the floor. Each eruption from his virgin body seemed more powerful than the last, and we both watched in awe as the bathroom was splattered with his cum. Finally emptied, he then washed the tip of his penis.

"This is the first time this has ever happened," he marveled, and I believed him.

Before he had time to tie up his *shalwar*, I told him I wanted to take a better look. I examined his now-flaccid penis and balls, then asked him to turn around.

"No," he protested, but by now his refusal was weak, and he turned his back to me.

His perfect peach-shaped buttocks were smooth.

"Bend down. I want to take a closer look."

I reached out and gently spread his cheeks, taking my first glimpse of an asshole. As he felt my fingers working to spread out his ass, he instantly straightened up and refused to bend down again for me, rejecting my pleading.

"No, no," he protested. "Not there."

Obviously, this exploration had started to alarm him. Though this was new to me, he clearly knew from his experience that assholes have uses other than defecation, and that by presenting his asshole for inspection he ran certain risks. Perhaps he knew, through experience or anecdote, that assholes were designed for entry by penises in addition to egress feces, and was unwilling to expose his rear portal to my curiosity.

"Please," I beseeched, "just to look."

Again he turned around, bent slightly, and spread his cheeks. I gazed at what to my memory must have been the perfect asshole, symmetric and furrowed, peach pink and pristine. I knew somehow that this was a significant and monumental part of his anatomy, of a man. I reached out with my finger, and lightly touched the funnel of his sphincter. Instantly, his muscles clamped down. He swiftly straightened up, tied his *shalwar*, and said he had to go.

He departed, but the memory of his asshole remains. My fascination with it was my first indication that I wanted to get deeper into that section of a man. It was much later that I made the connection between the orifice that I had seen, touched, and felt clamp down on my probing finger, and my desire to thrust into it, to open it, and to investigate it as a gateway to satisfaction.

Action On The Sidelines: Kushti

Idle curiosity fueled my empirical investigation into the sexuality of men at this stage of my development. I would seek out men, or public gatherings of men, in an instinctive search. One such excursion led to my discovery at the age of fourteen of the *kushti*,[1] or free-form wrestling matches, which were a common evening gathering place for workingmen.

Most men work a six-day week, so that the evening of the sixth day is very special. It is the only evening that a man can take off and stay out late if he wishes. He can go out with friends to a park or the beach, take part in team sports, or simply watch *kushti* with other men. Single men usually have no-

---

[1] Most informal *kushti* bouts are strictly for men and technically for entertainment, recreation and competition, though bets are made and money changes hands. A man may take his family to the beach at Clifton, for example, on the seventh day, which is now Friday, the Muslim holiday.

where they have to be, so watching a *kushti* match provides a diversion. For family men, this was their only evening off from the obligations of wives, children, and perhaps other family members who occupied the household.

A favorite gathering spot for *kushti* was a stretch of vacant land near our house and within sight of the ocean. I discovered it quite by accident one evening as I was bicycling by one late afternoon. Though the sun had lost its fire to the cooler evening breeze; the slow onset of dusk meant several more hours of light.

A large crowd of men and boys gathered in a circle around a makeshift ring as the appointed hour approached. The field of action was a circular area near the center of the vacant plot, measuring perhaps twenty feet in diameter, which had been cleared of stones, sticks, and other debris, and the dirt flattened. This served as the ring, around which the first circle of men crowded at the periphery.

The contestants stripped down to tight briefs for their matches, and entered the ring. There would be several bouts tonight, encouraged by the crowd's loud cheering, and probably, prize money. For the men in the ring, there were few rules and plenty of physical contact. All eyes were on the contestants, as men squirmed to fill available space and stood on tiptoe to glimpse the action.

Packed in behind this first circle of spectators were additional layers of spirited men and boys, cheering, yelling instructions and encouragement to their favorite fighter. In the middle of a particularly close match, this orderly perimeter would be breached as, unable to contain their enthusiasm, men would push each other to get a better view of the action. For those sandwiched in between the layers, the aroma of masculine sweat and grime was pervasive. Men would drape arms around their male companions. Men were pressed against men, all straining to get a better view, bodies angled and entwined, screams of delight as the dry dust of the ring billowed and a contestant was wrestled to the ground.

What first caught my attention was that between bouts and even during the match, some men on the periphery would frequently glance around while fondling their genitals. This is not an unusual sight in itself. Men often play with or scratch their genitals in public. One advantage of the *shalwar-kameez*, and even more so of the *dhoti*, is the freedom accorded to the genitals. Penis and testicles hang freely and are easily accessible.

Then what caught my eye was The Look. This is the universal glance that men give men when men want men. I have seen it described in a hundred different ways, cultivated phrases to express the signals of desire that emanate from a man when he is ready for democratic sexual contact with his fellow man. This Look spans continents and cultures, and time stands still when there lurks the possibility of wandering within its radiance. Antennae that can pick up the Look are grafted within us and, as children of the Look, we find its magic revealed to us in stages, with experience. Investigating the Look requires empirical practice. The Look is part visual contact, part stance, and part the projection of presence. But dissecting it into its components brings no satisfaction, just as the inventory of the electronics in an audio receiver provides little clue to the melodious strains it can evoke. Just as beautiful electronics can make bad music, and a properly tuned, aging receiver can convey flawless audio radiance, so it is that the Look silently transforms the ordinary man into a prospective sex organ from top to toe.

In this gathering, I felt the Look, though I saw little out of the ordinary. I knew, without the proper application of the rules of evidence, that there were many within this group who were in silent partnership with me, and who were radiating on the same frequency. Without knowing who or where or how or why, I just knew. I was wirelessly connected to them and, without knowing why or what, I was driven inexorably to meet them. In that dusty plain where I rode my bicycle lay new discoveries that I had no choice but to make.

He was in his twenties, nattily dressed in a clean *shalwar-kameez*. His eyes would casually dart around from time to time, looking at members of the audience rather than at the wrestlers. Occasionally, his hand would move to his crotch and his fingers would fondle his penis. Though he was several feet away from me, I knew instinctively that he had been afflicted by a special condition. Later, I would know that this was named "horniness."

He cast the Look in my direction. With my bicycle under my left arm, I edged my way closer. He was plain looking, but too well fed to be working class, with cheeks that were full and round, and bushy eyebrows that bridged his finely shaped nose. His skin was a dark natural olive, unburnt by the sun. I deduced that he lived in one of the nearby houses and had come here in search of sport. This made me more comfortable, since his behavior in his own neighborhood was likely to be more predictable, more constrained by the conventions of decorum. He would be discreet in whatever he did, since he was unlikely to want to attract public attention. A rough peasant or servant could try to take advantage of whatever situation developed. Instinctively, I felt that he was within my class, though perhaps a notch or two below.

I edged my way near him and positioned myself so that my arm hung a few inches in front of his crotch. He was not very tall, so his crotch was at the level of my wrist. I maneuvered an "accidental" brush against his bulge. A chill went through me, and I froze, rigid, and held my breath. Did he know that this was no accident? Or would I have the gall, the brazen temerity, to try again?

I need not have worried, because the tableau had been set for our *pas de deux*. He moved forward, so that my bare arm lightly pressed against his penis, beneath the cloth of both his *kameez* and his *shalwar*. I didn't flinch or move away. He maintained contact for a few moments to be sure, then slowly pressed forward more firmly against my arm. His penis was now horizontally erect under his loose clothes. He pressed its side against my arm, moving slowly back and forth against my wrist with some urgency. In turn, I rubbed my wrist back and forth against his stout, solid penis, and let it linger near its head, my instincts telling me that this was the pinnacle. Boldly, I wedged our bodies to hide the contact point, turned my hand and stroked his very fat and substantial organ. It was daylight in a public place, and we had not yet seen each other face to face at close range. Indeed, what was there to say?

The urgency of his thrusts mounted, as I my fingers played with the head of his penis, then lightly ran down the shaft. He squirmed. I could feel his quickening breath against my nape. Though my ministrations were obviously arousing him, I still did not know what direction this arousal would take, except that he was now starting to lose control. He was pressed securely against me, my hand continuing to work his cock. As his passions mounted, his entire body was starting to quiver.

Surely others could see! A bout had just ended and men around us were shifting their positions, moving and shouting in jubilation or groaning complaints. People were looking around, freed from the focal point of the field. Amid this motion, my partner and I stood still as though nothing had changed, coupled and immobile. The head of his penis was dribbling against my palm, and I knew this moment somehow had to end.

I panicked. In an instant, I turned my bike around, darted away, mounted my bike and rode off. I glanced back and spotted him, looking surprised and disappointed by my departure, his *kameez* flaring at the front. His hand was under his *kameez*, evidently holding his dick, and his face had a beseeching look. We looked at each other briefly from a distance, and I sped away.

I rode around the block, away from the circle of men, their odors, and the heat of their flesh, to catch my breath and slow my excited heartbeat. Could I simply leave this congregation and return home? Scared, I was also strangely excited, captivated by this group of strangers. Each one of these men had penises under their garments—flaccid organs, fat, thin, long, short, stout, and tapered . . . and just as that man and I had joined each other for a few fleeting moments of union, so were all these other men potential partners. It felt so natural to be close to a man in heat, a heat manifest in his erection. I felt a torrid desire for further connection of this kind. While I was free of this man's penis, I was not at liberty to leave. The magnetic magic of the crowd had trapped me. A sense of wild exhilaration suffused me, and I could not resist the urge to return to the action. There was something deeply human, yet primal and unrehearsed, in what I had just experienced.

I peddled back the other side of the large circle of men, dismounted, and chained it securely to a gate. Worming my way into the crowd, men pressed me from the front and the back. For a few moments, I watched with flushed disquiet the arena where glistening male bodies wrestled. I thought I would just stand and watch the spectacle, in the company of all these men. I did not expect anything more to happen, though I looked around occasionally to assess the crowd.

Suddenly a man standing just behind me pressed his hard, flat belly against my elbow. He must have seen me looking around, and decided to take the chance. The bulge of his penis touched my hand momentarily. He was wearing a *dhoti*, so that there were just one layer of cloth around him. Though his penis was hanging straight down toward the ground, it was tumescent, as though gravity had won in the face of desire. My hand stayed pressed against his firm, full, cucumber-shaped organ, and he seemed content just to maintain this contact. The next wrestling match had now started, and all attention was fixed to the field. Moments passed, and both the man and I ascertained that this was an acceptable plateau of intimacy for us. Then, with one swift motion I deftly moved my fingers to open the folds of his *dhoti* and cup the head of his penis in my hand. It was at hand level, comfortable. Now, it was flesh touching flesh. This male appendage warmed the palm of my hand, and its heat focused all my senses on the contact point of my flesh to his. Nothing else seemed to matter: the crowd's gruff yells, the dust, the sweat and grime, the wild cawing of crows feasting on decaying garbage, the unmuffled roar of rickshaws and buses driving by exhaling noise and smoke—all receded to the background, all was just a gaudy tableau, a substitute for the reality that I held in my sweaty palm, the hard rod that was the pivot to the man behind me, yet unseen, who in turn was the fulcrum on which the world conducted its affairs. So long as I held this power in my hand, did anything else really matter?

His erection hardened as I stroked the head of his penis. I caressed the head and shaft with my fingertips. Around us, other men pressed in, cheering the contestants, since another bout had just ended. We stood silent and still, connected. In retrospect, I have to believe that this connection was evident to others. Yet, I felt that we were in a space that was totally private.

Moving only my fingers and my hand, I rhythmically massaged his penis' head. His breath quickened, but his body was still. Moments later, I felt liquid seep into my hand, and drip down to the dusty soil below. I wiped my hand on the cloth of his *dhoti*, and withdrew it, breaking our connection. I felt his hand reach out and clasp mine. For a moment, he squeezed it tightly, gratefully. I suddenly felt the urge to leave him and, as I turned, we caught our first glimpse of each other. He was an older man, perhaps in his fifties, with salt-and-pepper hair. His face was furrowed from worry and work; his clothes were clean but unkempt. This was Friday, so he may have just come from the mosque after the traditional communal Friday prayers.[1] His sad glance was grateful. I walked away from the crowd without looking around any further and retrieved my bicycle. I felt strangely satisfied. I had had enough for a day.

Meanwhile, my earlier quarry had become a hunter. I glimpsed him as he circled the perimeter of the circle of spectators looking for someone to continue where I had left off. He spotted me and beckoned with a toss of his head. Tempted, I slowed down my departure, looked towards him to gauge his intentions. He began to walk away, looking back with gestures for me to follow. I showed my interest by bicycling slowly in the direction he was walking but keeping my distance. As we left the crowd, it became apparent that he was guiding me towards a more private place, but this was more than I was ready to handle. Without the protection of the crowd, I did not know what to expect if I took this any further. Fear overtook me. The next time he turned around to verify that I was still following, I shook my head, abruptly turned my bicycle, and rode furiously home, as though I was being chased. My day's adven-

---

[1] Friday is the day for communal prayer.

ture was done, and I had just advanced a step further towards understanding the mystery of my desire.

Adolescence and a New Emergence

Dramatic changes transformed my life as I entered adolescence, late, at sixteen years of age. These changes shook me out of my childhood torpor and ushered in a new phase of life, with the promise of a more interesting trajectory.

Perhaps most important, my health improved. I was now attending school with greater regularity. From an average of two months a year at school, I was now well enough to go to class for most of the school year, with only a few days off sick. This meant greater continuity with my few school friends, better integration into the academic curriculum, and the opportunity to leave the isolation of home. I also found that my weight was being naturally redistributed, so that I did not look as chubby. I was becoming better proportioned. I found muscles emerging where previously there had been only fat. A chubby child was becoming a young adult.

My outlook on life brightened as I gained new appreciation for the world around me. A shy child, I found it easier to spend this time at school studying, rather than attempting to participate socially. This put me in the comfortable company of other introverts, and I was faced with challenges that could be conveniently structured. Academic work, after all, was a simple matter of reading, memorizing, and taking examinations, without the daunting complexities of relationship-building.

I discovered that with a little study I could do quite well in school, and my academic improvement was quite dramatic. In a single year, I was able to leap from being close to the bottom of my class to being among the top three. This was tangible feedback, evidence of a direct relationship between effort and measurable result, and a good way to establish a position for myself within the institution. Other boys had a variety of interests—a mix of sports, extracurricular activities, studies, and social pursuits. By focusing on my studies, I found that I could identify with the bookworms. The others reasonably assumed that this was a conscious choice on my part, a chosen alternative to sports and social activity.

St. Patrick's school is among the better schools in Karachi. It is a Christian school, like its better-known Anglican counterpart, the Karachi Grammar School. Teaching standards were high when I attended and rigorously applied. Punctuality was required and discipline administered with the firm conviction of English public schools. Boys would be caned for infractions of the rules. An offender would be summoned to the front of the class, asked to bend down, and then whacked several times on his buttocks with a long, thin wooden cane that often splintered in the process. Of course, I was never at risk for such discipline. An outstanding student, I was the role model to whom the parents of naughty boys pointed, as they scolded their hormone-high adolescents for acts of mischief. Most of the boys, however, were less interested in studies than in the stirrings of adulthood.

The school was unisex and, under the facade of quasi-military discipline, there were hundreds of barely pubescent penises quivering rigidly towards their first orgasms, experimenting with the feel of tumescent flesh confined within the rough cloth of ill-cut regulation school uniforms. Inevitably, flesh was rubbed against flesh. Boys everywhere were starting to take matters into their own hands. Instant and uncontrollable erections abounded, and boys would walk around the school with their hands in their pockets, grasping their rude and as yet untamed members. There was even a term for it that came into popular use: "pocket billiards." Boys would jokingly point to another boy who, caught hand-in-pocket and clearly playing with himself, would blush as they laughingly accused him of playing this universal game. Sexuality was taking root in the halls of academia. As school became more central to my life, the laboratory for my experiments with sexuality moved here.

It was obvious to me that much of this sexual horseplay was taking place under the guise of sports. Boys would grab each other's crotches in the heat of competition. Even in social conversation, in the midst of banter, one boy would "finger" another, by making a grab for his genitals. The subject of this grab would then return the favor, and a tussle would ensue, and occasionally a mock fight, which was often just a wrestling bout with the crotch as booty. The "winner" would grab the other boy's genitals, and threaten to squeeze and not let go until the other boy "gave up." The victor handled the spoils with firm tenderness, and the vanquished took his time to declare defeat. The grabbed boy would often have an erection, so that there would be something to grab, or he would be wearing his pants tight, so that his genitals were visibly packaged, taunting other boys to feel them.

I avoided the sports field, but even the bookish among us were not immune to erotic urges. My friends and I stood in sedate clumps near the playing field, discussing homework assignments and ignoring the rough-and-tumble banter of our academic inferiors. However, though the imperatives of raging hormones coursed through our veins, physical contact was more difficult to initiate.

Mohammad was one of my close friends. He has since become a major banker in Karachi, but then he was a scrawny kid with large, clear eyes and a charming smile. While I was shy, he was outgoing, charming, and mischievous. His antics irritated and annoyed the more disciplinarian teachers, but he was always able to charm his way out of difficult situations. We found ourselves attracted to each other, but had so far interacted only in groups.

Mohammad's father was a mid-level bureaucrat, and the very large extended family that he supported was not well off. This showed in the quality of Mohammad's dress: his ill-cut uniform-quality trousers rode high to his ankles, and his crotch was too tight. He did not wear underwear,[1] so that the smooth curve of his balls could be clearly distinguished from the soft lump of his flaccid penis.

One day we were standing in the library, looking through books together for a class assignment. On this day the library was deserted, except for the librarian, who sat at her desk near the entrance. She was a middle-aged, black-skinned Christian[2] matron with an imposing figure and a fierce look. She was near the end of her day, and it was clear that she would not move from her perch unless she had to. I was standing by Mohammad, and we were both facing her. He turned towards me, so that my hand was now near his crotch. Perhaps he initiated it, or I may have taken the lead, but my hand grazed his flaccid penis. He did not move. Instead, he pressed it harder against my hand, and I could feel its swell towards erection. What we were now doing was unmistakable.

---

[1] It is not unusual for children, and even men, to wear trousers without underwear. The weather is hot and humid, and good genital ventilation reduces the likelihood of skin ailments like "prickly heat" and other rashes.

[2] St. Partick's is a Christian school and most employees were Christian. The Christian minority in Pakistan was converted by missionaries, primarily from the lower Hindu castes. These lower castes are generally darker skinned, and conversion afforded them an escape from the Hindu caste system.

I held the back of my hand against his penis, and it continued to grow, to fill out like an awakened snake ready to pounce. Throughout this we feigned studying, nervously monitoring the oblivious librarian, though what we were doing was hidden from her view by the high table that stood between us and her.

I ran the back of my hand across the length of his cock, and his now-stationary body quivered. I turned my hand around, so that his hard cock filled my palm. I could feel his rigid shaft, capped by an equally rigid head, confined by his tight pants. He pressed against me, rocking his hips, pinning my wrist to the table's edge. His hand braced his taut body against an adjacent bookcase. The urgency of his motions begged me not to stop.

With a swift, expert motion, I unzipped his trousers and, with one quick movement, he released his hard, fat cock into my grasp. I looked down, flushed by what I had done. His liberated penis strained against my hand, its shaft straight and thick, pressed into my palm. We had not yet glanced at each other. His eyes were glued to the page on the book we were studying, while his body was trembling as he barely breathed. I stroked his erection more boldly, and as his excitement elevated, he turned his body so that his cock was pointed away from me and toward the solid teak bookcase. Mohammad again checked out the librarian, who was still deeply absorbed in reading the magazine. I followed his gaze, and then we looked at each other. His face was alive, his eyes bright with animal desire, which I was stoking by manipulating his sexual tool. I quickened my strokes as he rammed his dick into the imaginary hole made by my clasping fingers. Within moments he heaved his ejaculation. Powerful squirts drenched the varnished wood with jets of thick white cum that cascaded down the side of the bookcase towards the floor. There they filled the tile edges with pools of viscous, bright white liquid. I continued stroking his still-rigid dick, until he pushed my hand away. Then he put his equipment back in its cradle and zipped up its protective cover. As if distancing ourselves from the evidence of our indiscretion, we moved to another table, remaining there long enough to feel calm, and then we left the library. As we exited, Mohammad mumbled that he had to go home and, as he turned toward me to formalize our good-bye, I caught a glimpse of his crotch, which had a large wet mark where cum had continued to seep out.

We never spoke of the event, nor was it ever repeated. The incident did not bring us closer, nor did it appear to affect our relationship.

Through the past thirty years since we were graduated, I lost touch with Mohammad but learned that he had married, was raising a large family, and had become very fat and very rich. A few years back I met him at a Karachi wedding reception, and he described to me his recent quadruple bypass operation in London, done by a famous Harley Street surgeon who had advised him to reduce his caloric intake.

He laughed: "I left the hospital and immediately had a full dinner. I love rich food, *chawal* and *paratha* and *saalan*. What is a meal without *mithai*?[1] If there is another problem with my heart, I am not worried. I have the best doctors. They will take care of me. That is their job. I must live well, otherwise what is the point? It is up to God to decide when I have to die and that

---

[1] *Chawal* is rice. *Paratha* is flat-fried unleavened bread, often stuffed with potatoes or meat. *Saalan* is a spicy food, like curry. *Mithai* are sweets, also known as "sweetmeats."

my family is well taken care of." He died of a heart attack less than a month later.

༺ ༻

In a spectacular incident at school, two boys had been expelled. They had been caught in the boys' toilet. Rumor had it that a janitor had walked in and found the younger boy bent over with the older boy pumping into his behind. Both had been immediately escorted to the principal's office, where the sordid copulation had been described and tearfully admitted. Their parents were informed, and the boys were instantly ejected. The following day, all students were subjected to a lecture on morality. The principal talked about discipline, about the need for boys to be careful and not dishonor the school, their parents, and their community. Sex wasn't mentioned, lust was not discussed, but every boy present knew what we were being warned about.

During this period, one of my good friends was a small, bookish boy named Aziz. He was frail, generally morose, and timid. We would spend hours together. His mother would sometimes ask my advice about what to do about him. Since he was not a very good student, she secretly hoped that spending time with me would be good for him and that he would learn by osmosis, or at least develop better study habits and test-taking skills.

We were often in my room chatting, and I found his rather melancholy outlook on life to be a refreshing alternative to the bluster and attitude that was more often typical among my more extroverted peers. Aziz and I talked about life and its meaning and about books. We discussed ideas and philosophies. He was an avid reader, and we found that we had several authors we admired in common. We were raising the same questions, and were confronting the same lack of answers: Did God exist? How should society be structured? What was the meaning of life? He was neither overtly sexual nor sensual, but since I was one of his few friends, I could count on his constant availability. I simply had to ask for him, and he would visit.

One day we were both in good spirits and started horsing around. Before too long, we were on the floor of my bedroom, our limbs entwined, wrestling playfully. My hand was on his knee, and my arm was pressed against his crotch. His hand was pushing my inner thigh, its back pressed against my genitals. Suddenly, we stopped tussling and remained motionless, without untangling ourselves. My nose was buried in his hair just above his ear, and I could smell his sweaty scalp. It was a warm, mulchy, male smell, mixed in with the lingering aroma of incompletely rinsed shampoo. It felt just fine. His head lay on my chest. By silent mutual consent, we relaxed our muscles and loosened our grips on each other and stayed close. I could feel my cock harden and felt his respond against my leg. Boldly, I moved my arm to caress him. He stayed still. We lay with each other like this for several minutes, limbs nestled in quiet intimacy. Reluctantly, we moved away from each other in silent mutual consent. As we stood up, I had a hard-on. Aziz gently pressed his thigh against my hard-on, and we stood this way for some time—his small ass just a slight thrust away. I believe he wanted me to make the next move but in my conventionality and timidity, I lacked the necessary confidence. He wanted to be fucked, and I was not ready. It was one thing to play with the hard dicks of servants and a major step forward to jerk off a classmate in a library, but this seemed to be uncharted territory, especially with a classmate I would have to face again the following day. I pressed my erection hard against his soft butt, embraced him, then backed away and turned around. A knock on the door broke the tension, and we turned to other matters.

෮෬

The period of my life between sixteen and eighteen went by in a blur. I was now developing an identity, a sense of self anchored in academic accomplishment. I no longer had time to waste. The curriculum at school emphasized test-taking and rote learning, so that I would meet with classmates in study groups, and much of the time was actually spent studying. I was starting to discover the world, and it was unfolding as an exciting adventure.

This was also a relatively asexual period for me, because schoolwork took center stage. There was work to do. I studied with friends who were as academically inclined, and we intensely compared notes, as we charted our careers. There was little time to spend socializing, as the academic course work was quite demanding.

My school had an excellent academic reputation. The best students in school could take advanced exams that were required to apply to universities abroad. Since I was now among this select group, I sat for these exams, and did quite well. I was now encouraged, especially by my grandmother, to take the SAT,[1] which are used for admission to U.S. colleges. My results were well above average, so that it made sense to apply to universities in the United States of America. I did not really expect to follow through if I gained admission. This was all process and procedure, something that the better students did because of peer pressure, as a matter of course. Besides, I thought that my poor health made me an unlikely candidate for travel abroad.

---

[1] Scholastic Aptitude Test.

While my parents and grandmother encouraged me, my grandmother was concerned that my health would make it difficult for me to be able to survive the cold winters of North America.

My apparently bright prospects also helped to improve my relationship with my father. He acknowledged my academic achievement and was proud to show me off to his peers, many of whom had sons who were less successful academically. I attained a position of some respect in the household, and greater visibility. I was the first to face the prospect of leaving the family, and this brought us closer together. While my older brother had only recently left the house, he had in some sense been gone a long time. At twenty-three, he was married and already had his first child (a daughter). He had settled in Islamabad and worked as a trainee at a government job.

My grandmother was quite selfless in her dedication to my future success. Despite concerns about my health in a distant land, she encouraged me every step of the way. She promoted my self-esteem, which was still low from my isolated childhood and distant family life. Even though it meant leaving her and departing Karachi, she encouraged me to aim high.

Events were moving ahead at dizzying speed, and before too long I was selecting from, and negotiating with, the various universities that had made me offers of admission.

Among the colleges that admitted me was Columbia University, in New York City. It also awarded me scholarship money to cover tuition and expenses, so there seemed to be little standing in the way. I had gained admission to a prestigious college, and that was cause for pride and celebration. Thus began the next great transition in my life, from Pakistan to North America.

At the age of eighteen, I boarded a plane to New York. There I was met by some Pakistani friends of friends, who quickly absorbed me into the extended family of expatriates in the New York area. From a relatively secular and secure family life, I was thrust into the harsh and freewheeling world of New York, where values and roles, meanings and intellect, were constantly challenged and debated. The Pakistani community was conservative and family oriented but, within it, I found security, comfort, and connection with roots I never knew I had before I left.

Since I was a newcomer, I had much to learn about life in the U.S. New York was a great teacher. Living alone and with roommates, I learned for the first time what I had taken for granted, from having to wash my own clothes, to dealing with very different cultural assumptions. Underground, even to myself, the seeds of my sexuality continued to mature, but it would be some time before they would sprout through the surface.

Within a few weeks after I left, my grandmother had a stroke and died. I think it was from a broken heart, at seeing me leave and knowing that I would never be close with her again. She had insisted that I leave to pursue my education, though it must have been extremely painful for her to see me go. I still treasure the letters she wrote to me, the advice and encouragement she continued to give until the day I left, and her exhortation that I set high goals for myself. Her last letter quoted a verse, translated from Persian, of which she was particularly fond:

> *Stand upright, speak your thoughts, declare*
> *Speak out the truth, that all may share*
> *Be bold, proclaim it everywhere*
> *They only live who dare.*

The Puzzling New World

The intense and competitive environment at Columbia was intimidating. As a shy and bookish foreign student, I found the social environment a greater challenge than the course work. It was bewildering to watch extroverted American students speak up in class when they had nothing to say and teachers intentionally pose questions for which there were no answers. I found myself slowly learning how to think critically, how to structure and solve problems, and how to hold my ground in abstract intellectual discussions.

The immodesty of the men around me was a dramatic change from my previous experience. Men in Pakistan are fully clothed most of the time. Even at home, most men would not consider wearing shorts, or removing their shirts. In the hot sun, the best way to stay cool is to wear loose clothing, so that all that is visible is the face and hands. Certainly, men do not expose their bodies to other men when changing, bathing, or at any other time. There are no communal showers, and no opportunity to see naked men. Modesty is a necessary part of being *shareef*,[1] too natural to be conscious.

In the U.S. I saw men naked for the first time. Casually, unceremoniously, my fellow students would strip down and walk into the shower, absolutely naked! Penises dangling, balls hanging low, they would walk around uninhibitedly, talking as though they were fully dressed! And yet, when dressed, if they so much as brushed up against a friend, there would be an instant apology, as though a violation of some kind had occurred. In fact, they kept their distance from their fellows, suggesting to me that to get close would be an unacceptable intrusion.

In Pakistan the opposite is true. Men walk down the street hand-in-hand. They embrace, sit with arms and legs entwined, and freely touch each other to make a point. Touching is seen as a sign of affection, a natural accompaniment to a gesture, or to a spoken word. There is nothing sexual about physical intimacy, although there are strict unwritten rules that govern it: for example, no contact below the waist in an embrace.

Men in Pakistan dress and shower in privacy, since to expose their genitals is seen as immodest, rude, and embarrassing. This is true even in all-male boarding schools, where communal shower stalls are fully enclosed for privacy. There is no acceptable public forum for nakedness, no display of asexual nudity to enable inspection of the male (or female) body.

I had the opportunity, then, to feast my eyes upon the naked male body as an object for the first time. I observed the male physique and began to take the next slow steps towards appreciating its beauty. I found myself drawn to parts other than the external, hanging genitals. The shoulders, the chest, the shape

---

[1] Respectable. *Sharafat* is associated with family honor, and is not to be compromised at any cost.

of men's legs and thighs. In motion, how beautiful! I found myself drawn to the smooth expanse of skin of the back, and admired the flare of the buttocks, and the cleavage in-between, the way the smooth flare of a well-developed chest would give way to the petulance of a belly button, which in turn led to the pubic area.

And cocks, dicks, penises! So many, in such variety. Black and brown and yellow and white, small and majestic, shriveled and semitumescent, circumcised and uncircumcised. I would lie in wait outside the communal shower, as a particularly attractive student completed his shower. When I heard the sound of the water turning off, I would casually stroll in to urinate, and watch as he emerged nude from the shower stall to dress. I wanted to reach out and touch wet skin, to feel the body I watched in motion. But I didn't dare. There was no expression of feeling and affection in public between men, and it was quite clear to me that the naked male body was not to be construed as an erotic object.

With appreciation came discrimination. There were pimply buttocks, sallow chests, and ugly, flaccid penises. But even the men on which these were attached exuded their own attraction. I found that pale, white skin was not instinctively appealing to me. I also discovered my preference for well-proportioned men, and my sexual indifference to obese men, perhaps as a consequence of my father's and my own childhood battle with weight.

Most movies I saw as a child were English-language ones. The actors in these movies were superficially similar to these men. Curiously, however, I had never harbored erotic fantasies for these actors, though they had clearly been handsome men. I did not pass through an adolescent phase of erotic idol worship. I admired the Beatles, and I had memorized Elvis Presley's songs, but these were cultural icons in the Western-style subculture of my school environment. My erotic impulses blossomed through direct exploration and, in retrospect, my fantasy life was clearly underdeveloped. These naked men held no sexual interest for me *per se* and, since I presumed that I was not of erotic interest to them, my curiosity was that of a Peeping Tom.

Indeed, their nakedness was as lifeless as an image, as sexless as a photograph. They lacked sensuality, their eyes were opaque to me. In turn, I approached them with a sensible businesslike demeanor. Like beautiful automatons, these naked men paraded about the lockers at the gym, dried themselves unconcernedly while I watched from the side of my eye, and appeared quite oblivious to the potential for sexual contact. None of them looked at me with the slightest hint of *shararat*.[1] None of them inspired me to erection, nor did they appear in my dreams at night.

Could I Be Gay?

It had never occurred to me to classify myself on the basis of my sexual desires. It was clear to me that I was sexually interested in men. However, it was equally clear that I was a man like the rest, and outwardly just as normal. My attraction to men was natural to me. I was not an identifiable *gandu*, nor did I feel abnormal. I knew I did not fall within the norm, however, and I kept my sexual interest in men secret. I assumed that I would eventually develop an adequate interest in women, get married, raise a family, and thereby continue along the "normal" track. However, I could not deny this fascination with men. At

---

[1] Playfulness, mischief. The term also connotes naughtiness.

that time, I did not know enough to feel the need to acknowledge that this orientation was generally classified as "gay." So far as I was concerned, this cognitive dissonance was perfectly natural to me, and I had complete confidence that I would adapt to it.

I saw in the campus newspaper that a gay group was seeking recognition on campus as a legitimate student activity. This was in the early seventies, and gay rights had not yet established a beachhead of legitimacy. Occasionally, articles would be published on the subject, but this was seen by my mainstream classmates as part of the zaniness of the period, guerrilla theater in keeping with the times. Gay rights were not even a controversial issue yet. However, opposition to the Vietnam war was at its zenith, and the resistance movement was at its peak. It seemed only fair to me to give homosexual men (no women were mentioned) their day in court, along with Black Panthers, SDS (Students for a Democratic Society), and Marxist groups, and free love advocates.

The article mentioned that this proposal would be presented and discussed at the next meeting of the student council. I went to this meeting.

I had read enough books about homosexuality by now to know that the gay group was talking about an aspect of me. I knew almost by heart the HQ76 section of the Library of Congress classification. I had discovered André Gide's *Corydon*, the Marquis de Sade's complete works, all of Jean Genet's books, James Baldwin, and Somerset "Auntie" Maugham—so nicknamed by his nephew Robin Maugham, who was also homosexual. Now I wanted to see the brave man who had organized this group and who had the courage to stand up in front of his peers and openly declare he was gay! What would he look like? Would he be a flamboyant queen, marked instantly by his "perversion"? This would be my first glimpse into that window of the gay world that I didn't realize was a mirror. I thought it would be interesting to observe someone who stood up and labeled himself.

I had not yet assimilated the American obsession with categories and labels, whether ethnic, racial, gender, or political. Since the mind can contain only a finite number of descriptive labels, if there is one label per dimension, a person can be reduced to a few major dimensions. Manageable, perhaps, but not very interesting. A "commie pinko fag" is forever forbidden from having anything in common with a "right-wing racist breeder," since their labels don't overlap. I have always felt a horror at the way labels throttle the generous humanity within us all. They are to be used sparingly, and only to achieve specific goals, such as for political gain. This applies as much to the word "gay" as to any other identifier. To me, I was *who* I was, and "branding" myself for the convenience of others seemed odd. Nevertheless, even then, I knew that the man who organized this gay group and I shared something in common.

He called himself Terry and was disappointingly ordinary in appearance. I had hoped that he would perhaps be distinctive in some way, perhaps even attractive to me. He made his presentation with simplicity and sincerity, saying he wanted to form a gay students' union on campus to provide support for other gay men and lesbians and to educate students about gayness. After his advertisement in the campus newspaper had appeared, he had received twenty calls from interested people. He was clearly speaking from his heart, and the assembled student representatives voted to establish the organization.

I felt an instant affinity with Terry, though I did not find him attractive in the least. In fact, though I found some of the men around me attractive in a general sort of way, at this stage

I did not lust after any of them. I was still investigating the nature of my desire, and my search for answers through reading was a far more comfortable method for me than contact with a real person. I needed to know who I was, what was known about this "condition," and who else was this way. My voracious reading of the medical and research literature had left me unsatisfied. There was much research and study of homosexuality, and I read through the literature in the library with great dedication, despairing that I did not find any real connections between what I read and my reality. Researchers and sociologists like Havelock, Albert Ellis, Bieber, and Socarides, talked of a breed that I felt I did not belong to. These were analysts, sociologists, and clinicians, who discussed homosexuality as a propensity that qualified men and women for inclusion in a deviant group known as "homosexuals." Once grouped, homosexuals could be studied in various ways. Homosexuals were subject to the terrifying power of the scientific method, misapplied. Jews, blacks, and other groups have from time to time been subject to "scientific" analysis that identified statistical variations between their characteristics as a group and the "normal" mainstream. Homosexuals were similarly scrutinized by these sociologists and others like them. Whatever the motivation of the authors, generalized conclusions about living people, grouped by singular characteristics, are rarely confined to the detached debate of rarefied intellectual circles. Almost inevitably, as with blacks and Jews, there is a demand for public policy changes to insulate the mainstream and to return these pathetic and wretched deviants to normalcy, and save them if possible. During this period, psychiatrists, sociologists, researchers, and others sought to rescue homosexuals through electric shock aversion therapy, excluding them from jobs, terrorizing gay bars, trapping them in pickup spots, excluding them from the country, and damning their souls from the pulpit. The sordid intellectual foundation for this exercise was every bit as heinous as the assertions of William Shockley about the inferiority of blacks, or the Nazis' pronouncements about the Jews. We emerged from that era only through valiant battles, fought by thousands of foot soldiers who dismantled this categorization, rescued the individuality of each of us, and laid the foundation for political strength through the gay movement.

Sterile academic conclusions sanctioned the practice of cruelty. In seeking to test the hypothesis that homosexual desire could be cured, vulnerable young men tormented with socially unsuitable sexual desires were made victims of their confessions. Strapped to chairs, with electric wires connected to their penises, they were shown erotic pictures of men. When they responded with erections, volts of electricity, milliamps of electric current, were used to still their desire. Their screams of pain did not cure them. This "aversion therapy" is just one example of the horrors visited on homosexuals in the past.

At the same time Kinsey, the famed sex researcher, published a sliding scale—at one end were perfect heterosexuals, at the other end were the irretrievable homosexuals—and he proclaimed that everyone else had proclivities in-between. Thus, there was latent homosexuality in most people. One book, *One in Twenty*, postulated that five percent of the population was homosexual. All these studies held sexual contact between men to be significant, noteworthy, and a valid basis for the classification of their subjects.

I instinctively rejected this basis for classifying myself, because I never assumed that what I did sexually was a significant enough part of my identity, though I understood that others could. There was an underlying set of moral assumptions in these texts that left me cold. There was an assumption that normal and good were synonymous, that being normal was significant and important, and that differences in sexual behavior were somehow more vital than differences in hair or skin color. There seemed to be a level of the analysis aimed at measuring deviance from some norm. But I was not a deviant; I did not feel like a deviant. Perhaps I was just an abnormal deviant, I wondered, punning from the mathematics I was studying. None of the books came close to directly confronting me with who I was: a normal person who happened to be attracted to men. Worse, I had no tools with which to sketch the dimensions of this desire. Rather than judge it, I wanted to understand it, and to build on it.

I felt despondent and isolated. Where I thought I had found a connection, there appeared to be none. I felt just as alone as during my childhood, distant and separated from the action. My childhood was spent in aloneness, and I accommodated to this disconnection by adapting. One element of this was the objectification of what others did. Since I was not part of the real world, I could separate what happened from my assessment of it. As I built a value framework within which to operate, I could judge the actions of others without the cloud of subjectivity. Others voiced opinions as participants, while I was able to connect an opinion to the underlying axioms. Within this frame, sexual acts were pleasurable, harmless, and therefore certainly not bad. Their connection to morality lay closer to the realm of ethics than to the realm of sentiment. I saw my sexual play with servants as an attempt to build a loving connection, construct a higher bridge of understanding, to render myself vulnerable to emotion and affection. It was not simply the rubbing of skin, culminating in cum.

I fancied that my secret universe would somehow unlock for me the meaning of community and family, beyond my biologically inherited one. What I found in my reading, however, was less than satisfying, even beyond the scientific segregation of "my type" for study. Sex was the basis for control, power, domination, and revenge. The entire sordid range of man-woman relationships of the "Harold Robbins"-type was mirrored in the gay world. Did Somerset and Robin Maugham really seduce boys in North Africa to establish a nobler connection, or was it pure colonial power? Did Jean Genet's tortured sexual tales contain romance and lyric, or was it all just the self-flagellation of a confused mind? Perhaps I admired Gore Vidal most, at this stage. He wrote well, his accounts seemed sincere, and he was able to integrate his distinguished family heritage with his search for a man to love. However, these were ultimately all bookish questions and conclusions, untested and unproven. They did, however, launch me into a search for self-discovery.

The campus newspapers started to report meetings of gay organizations. I would walk to and near these meetings, but never summoned up the courage to actually join a group. One meeting that I recall was at an old church near campus. It was a cold New York evening. The church was otherwise empty, and I walked up to the window to observe the crowd within. I stood outside the church door as the participants left after the meeting, laughing and talking amongst themselves.

"These people all call themselves gay," I thought. "This is what gay people look like!" They looked no different, and yet they were asserting a presumed difference. I could not fathom why. They seemed relaxed and happy, and I was again the outsider, looking in. But these men were true outsiders, stereotyped or shunned by the mainstream society they lived in. I could not afford public association with them, but yet I was drawn to them as though by a secret bond.

While I did not classify myself in any way, nor did I see the purpose of any such classification, those men clearly did. They understood that in free societies, self-classification addresses the social goal of a fair distribution of power and the establishments of rights and entitlements. I found such classifications unnecessary, and merely an impediment to an open set of options. I was a man, biologically. A Pakistani, as my passport stated. A Muslim by name and by birth. A student—and I had an ID to prove it. Beyond that, I saw no reason to categorize myself and voluntarily reduce my degrees of freedom.

I also could not construct in my mind the dialog I would have with one of these gay men. What would we talk about? Why would we have anything to talk about? After all, what did we have in common, anyway? The notion of gay sensibility was absent from my consciousness. I could not construct the framework within which to discuss my desires, nor the language with which to express them. Having read all the books in the university library on the subject, fully literate to a fault, I could still make no emotional connection between who I was and what these gay organizations represented. True, the literature talked of homosexuals, gay people, and issues relating to being gay. True, also, to some degree, I identified myself with this classification. But this identification was academic, disconnected from any type of natural next step: if I was homosexual/gay, then what did this mean for me, my life, and my world?

Absent emotion, the next lowest common denominator was lust. As with any well-defined commodity, lust was traded according to the laws of the free market. This was the era of the free street paper, and in New York these papers now sported a "men seeking men" section. So I decided on the practical step, and placed a personal ad with a post-office-box return address. Everything in my ad was false, except the basics of my desire;

my name and my background were disguised. This was to be a laboratory experiment.

> Foreign student, 22, horny, looking for a meaningful friendship with gentle, sincere and educated person. This is my first time. I am just starting to live.

Weeks later I was surprised to receive dozens of responses. I screened them for suitability, applying all the wrong criteria: Did they appear serious? Were they well educated? I failed to realize that these were not job applicants, but potential sex partners!

The Virtuoso Seduction

John, a graduate student of music, wrote me a well-crafted letter. His handwriting was precise calligraphy, and his turn of phrase was inviting. I called him.

He had a friendly voice. "Where are you from?"

"India," I lied.

"I thought so!" he said. "Why don't you come over to visit? We can have a glass of wine and just chat."

I accepted his invitation and approached his apartment with some trepidation. I had left behind my wallet, including all ID cards, and carried only a small amount of money with me. I did not know what to expect! I had identified myself as "Bert" to him on the phone, but assumed he would surely ask for my "real"—that is, "Indian" name! I had decided to call myself "Singh," if the need arose.

John opened the door to let me in and was a very pleasant, somewhat husky individual, who moved softly and nimbly with remarkable grace. He had clearly done this before and had all the basic tools of seduction arrayed in harmony. The lights were dimmed. Chopin played softly in the background. The sofa was deep and warm and inviting. He served red wine in crystal glasses, which made a pleasant clinking sound as he raised a toast to my arrival. I felt comfortable and relaxed in a social sense, without any of the tight tension that I presumed would be associated with such a prelude to anonymous sex.

We spent the next few minutes chatting about inanities. He was charming, impeccably dressed with a faint cloud of cologne around him. He moved with the grace of a gazelle, enchantingly craning his neck and fluttering his eyes from time to time, to make a point. He set out to impress me in an understated way. A musician, he showed me his name on the program of a university performance the previous week. He pointed out the tasteful works of art that he had collected and made casual reference to his knowledge of such things. John refilled our wine glasses, commented appreciatively about its light fruitiness, and moved closer to me. Our eyes were level and his face was composed. After a short, audible breath that exhaled perfume, John looked deeply at me and, with the mildest of eyelash flutters, leaned over and kissed me on the lips. He then moved back and said, with a slight smile, "You are nice."

I did not really know what to say. I told him, "Thank you," and sensing the direction of this conversation, apologized, "I have really not ever done this before." Strangely, I felt neither aroused nor alarmed.

"No problem," he said, "I will be very gentle. We will go to the bedroom; just get comfortable. I have some Vaseline. I will go very slowly. You won't feel a thing, except pleasure. It will not hurt, don't worry!"

So *that* was what was on his mind! He wanted to introduce his cock into my asshole! I had advertised for sex, and sex was what he was about to deliver. I had not specified an item on the menu of possibilities, and so he had made his choice. He was prepared to deflower a virgin in style! This was not the kind of sex I had intended. I suppose now that the alternative could have been to negotiate with him to put my cock up his asshole instead. However, though he was a nice chap, I had had no erotic feelings for him, and I really felt no temptation to experiment with him in this way, to break new sexual ground. There was no connection, sexual or otherwise, and he embodied complete insincerity beyond his lust.

I told him that perhaps we could do it some other time, that I was inexperienced and really did not feel like continuing. He persisted in his persuasive tone and then, to his credit, sighed and gave up. I finished my glass of wine, then left. I never did have to claim to be an Indian named "Singh."

Over the next several months I posted a series of similar advertisements, and met two more men. One was a black man from Harlem called "Red" for no discernible reason. He was gentle and good humored, and his easygoing approach to life contrasted sharply with my harried pace. With him, time seemed to stand still, and the present moment was paramount. He was active in the Black Power movement and was hostile and angry at society when we spoke about political matters over coffee. However, when we reached the bedroom, his bitterness seemed to evaporate and we lay together, naked in bed, playing and laughing. Being with him felt comfortable and communal, though we never did progress beyond mutual masturbation.

Our first sexual experience offered my first deep sexual kiss. He had a sweet-tasting mouth. Perhaps it was his musky cologne, or the facility with which his tongue roamed in my mouth, but I felt he exuded sensuality, and an easy intimacy in bed. Once I had learned the technique, I lost no time in exploring his mouth with my tongue; while his body tightened, he rewarded my ministrations with a deep moan of pleasure.

Red was hung like a horse and his erection was awesome. His orgasms were silent, quick, and frequent. The steady dribble of cum from the gaping hole at the end of his large cock told me when he had concluded his exertions, but he continued kissing, continued until my mouth was sore and I was pleasantly exhausted. We parted with no promises to call exchanged. We had had our moment together and had not found a reason to plan for another. I could not discern Red's character sufficiently to understand him, and concluded that he did not warrant the effort.

The second man I met through my advertisement was a Boston Irishman with pale white skin and a funky, frizzy look. His name was Sean. We met at a coffee shop near his apartment. Without sitting down to talk, as though through mutual agreement, we went directly to his apartment. Once inside, we undressed, and he stepped forward and embraced me, pressing his mouth on mine. His tongue flickered nervously into my mouth, but this was only as a transit stop. His mouth quickly moved lower and enveloped my erection. He was now in his area of expertise, and I must say that my first blow-job was among the best ever.

His mouth lingered, while his tongue licked and his head pumped, thrusting my erection all the way down his throat. Like a fully absorbed violinist, he concentrated on the movement at hand, and on the single-minded goal of making me wild with desire and of prolonging the moment. When my spasms of ejaculation finally subsided, he kept my penis in his mouth for a few moments, squeezing me dry before letting me go.

Sean wanted just sex. More narrowly, he simply wanted to suck me, and then to see how long he had to wait before he could do it again. There was earnest labor in his effort, as he jerked himself off while slurping on my cum with focused hunger. There was no connection between us, beyond this body link. When we were through, there was nothing to say, and there was no tenderness in his touch.

We said our good-byes, and I never saw him again.

Except for occasional transient contacts such as these, I did not act more broadly on my sexual impulses during this period. I had no clue how to cruise—in the university's Low Library or elsewhere. My university life and social framework did not permit much freedom, and a significant amount of time was spent simply "shooting the breeze" with friends at the dormitory, or keeping company with other Pakistanis.

There were a few good cooks in my group of Pakistani friends, and I have memories of the aroma of curried chicken wafting from dormitory rooms, laced with the beautiful and somewhat mournful voice of Lata Mangeshkar, or the love songs of Mohammad Rafi. There was indeed a sense of community within the Pakistani student corps, sharing memories of common experiences of Pakistan. These experiences were generally limited to memories of the physical environment and landmarks we recalled, since I had not known any of my newfound friends before my journey abroad. Still, they knew of Bohri Bazaar, the huge maze of shops and narrow streets in the center of Karachi; of Elphinstone Street, the elegant thoroughfare that led to Frere Hall, with its colonial spire and spacious gardens; of Clifton, Hawkes Bay, and Sandspit, the beach areas of Karachi; and of Keamari, the port of Karachi. Some had experienced Karachi's scorching, dusty summers, and were nostalgic for its stench-laden streets. They knew of its conventions and public holidays, of its beggars and its communities. Most of these friends had little in common with me, but in this strange land we were bound by the conventions of compatriots, and what we shared of our past meant more than our individual differences. There was the sense of instant fraternal intimacy that must develop between soldiers at war, but this was no Sacred Band of Thebes; the common journey we had undertaken called for individual academic success, to improve our value in the marriage market, and to meet family obligations. While some of these friendships endured beyond university and slowly dissolved over the years, they were largely relationships of convenience, to assuage loneliness and to indulge in moments of nostalgia. I felt I was one of them, just as normal in my needs as they were in theirs, and just as family-oriented. It was easy to pass.

As a stranger in this strange land, I was closeted in this largely self-contained womb. I knew what I wanted sexually, but my need was not strong enough for me to do much more than experiment periodically with men I met through advertisements. There were several concurrent dimensions to my self-discovery; my sexuality merely took its place in the queue. Academic work was demanding and, this being the 1970s, political and social issues were raised and debated in a ferocious and dedicated way among students—something new to me. I found the intellectual fresh air bracing, and enjoyed honing my skills at argument, and at learning of local and national issues and concerns. There was a wonderful disorder about the way the world was organized. This, combined with the immense amount of information freely available, let students constantly challenge the assumptions of life, construct hypothetical alternatives, and even test them out in the laboratory environment of the university and nearby communes. There were social and political movements in support of various causes—to legalize marijuana, to end the Viet Nam war, to promote peace, free love and free sex.

There was the hippie movement, which seemed to advocate all these things and more and theoretically was in support of gay liberation, which was emerging in those days as the Gay Pride Movement.

I tracked with detached interest the progress of the different gay groups and their activities around campus. There was a dance mixer arranged by one such group, and I hung around near the entrance, studiously watching the men arrive and leave. They appeared more different than similar; the cultural differences between us transcended sexuality, especially since they had announced an affiliation and I had not. All that aside, I was simply afraid of going in to the dance.

As with the other special-interest groups of that era, those that were deeply invested in the gay movement stood outside the mainstream. I met several of these men individually on a social basis, yet never revealing myself, playing the part of a sympathetic outsider, a role familiar to me. "Belonging" never held any great appeal, even less when weighed against the costs.

My reading and study had also persuaded me that, even if I were "gay," that there were few benefits to joining a group or proclaiming myself to be part of a movement. I saw such men marginalized, their social contacts narrowed, and their attention defocused by their political mission. I pondered the meaning of this in my academic cocoon.

There seemed to be a pragmatic rationale for the gay movement: men who desire men, like I did, classified themselves as "gay" in order to draw strength from their numbers. The exercise of this aggregated strength resulted in "pride." The result of group pride was the ability to energize, mobilize, and advance as individuals. This advance, in turn, allowed each individual to fulfill his higher needs for social acceptance, love, and self-actualization. I saw the need for this cycle, but did not seem to fit in naturally at any of the entry points. This presumed cycle was so dissociated from my mainstream university life that it could be marginalized and managed without any overt bearing on the rest of my routine.

Abraham Maslow, the famed psychologist, described a hierarchy of needs that man rises through. As basic needs are satisfied, men naturally strive for higher needs. The lowest needs on the totem pole are the minimal ones, such as for food and shelter. At the apex of the hierarchy is self-actualization, the ultimate, *nirvana*. It seems to me now that gay men must rise through a couple of extra layers in Maslow's hierarchy of needs, work harder as they work upward through this cycle. This hard work leaves many exhausted. They get stuck with celebrating their identity forever, *puer aeternus*. I have seen grown men with advanced academic degrees and significant accomplishments "come out," drop out, and wallow in the exhilaration of liberty until they are too exhausted for anything else. They are gay! They are free! But what then? Having found a social environment that is equally gay, they find themselves settling for lower personal standards, setting more modest goals, and leaving the bigger challenges of the world for others. Rather than build this articulation of identity into something bigger for the broader social good, some descend into a morass of self-absorption, like wounded warriors. Relegated to the leper colony of gay ghettos in major cities, their plaintive "coming out" cries cut no ice among the mainstream majority, except as a curiosity, since they are too worn out to systematically do the work needed to seize mainstream power using mainstream values. For some, gay identity becomes a defining mission that leads to accomplishments that can stand on their own. For others, it leads to companionship with people with whom they would otherwise have nothing in common, and distances them from those they would otherwise value. Such people pay a heavy price for this ultimate attainment of self-acceptance. However, can there be a road to self-actualization that circumvents self-acceptance?

A Band-Aid solution is to have one foot out of the closet and one securely inside. But this is perhaps the most exhausting option of all, because it requires duplicity at a very fundamental level. By showing a different face to each audience, the lonely actor succeeds only in applauding his own acting skill. When the curtain comes down, the masquerade must end. Psychologists say that abused children are the most adept at acting as required to please people they encounter in their search for love and acceptance. Perhaps growing up gay in a straight world is one such type of abuse. Perhaps my childhood, with its memories of loneliness and isolation, made such an act a relatively effortless one to implement. I had long felt that I was acting rather than living. Dissimulation was my "natural" mode.

At that time, during the turbulent seventies, I knew that the gay-rights movement was fundamentally important to me. It was clear that homosexuals were functional outcasts and equally clear that "liberation" was nowhere close at hand. Secret sexual encounters could not substitute for public relationships. I was awed by the courage of those who stood up and spoke out. They were my heroes, and I admired them from afar and silently wished them luck. I bought a book published by the American Civil Liberties Union, *The Rights of Gay People*. In keeping with my cowardice, it was buried among several other books purchased from the bookstore on a shopping trip. In this book, I read of Frank Kameny, who had gone to Washington to demand rights for homosexuals. He was also living in Manhattan. Filled with anxiety, I called his office from a public phone and asked to speak with him. An immigration question, I said. He came to the phone, and I haltingly told him that I was from abroad, and that

I wanted to know about immigration rules and homosexuals. He said that homosexuals were excluded, along with psychopaths and communists, but that he was fighting to change this. Trembling with emotion, I thanked him and concluded the call. He had talked about *me* and confirmed my assumptions that I was not wanted if I fit in this category. I was worthless in the eyes of U.S. society and its government, if I was homosexual.

On another occasion I traveled to Boston and found that the famous French writer, Jean Genet, denied a visa for his many defiant perversions, had secretly slipped across the Canadian border to support a Black Panther rally and would be speaking on the Harvard campus in Cambridge, across the Charles River from Boston. I went to see him speak, and at one point came face to face with him. Instinctively, I thrust a pen and a piece of paper in front of him and requested his autograph. After he had signed, he looked into my eyes—a haunting, deep and lost look of loneliness and despair, filled with memory and misgiving. His soulful look mirrored my mood. I, too, was caught up in this life, a lost chameleon without a color to call my own. I passed through a phase of deep angst, as I re-read his work and pondered on the meaning of life.

Race and Racism

From my first day on North American soil, it was apparent that most people were of a different race than I. It also became quickly apparent that race played a major part in how money, opportunity, and power were allocated. Since I am non-white, how did I perceive racism, and how did that relate to my sexuality?

Pakistan is also a race-conscious country. Families and some ethnic groups are readily identifiable by race and often classified as such. During the period that East Pakistan gained independence as Bangladesh, anti-Bengali racist comments were commonplace. Race-based stereotypes abounded about Sindhis, Punjabis, Memons, Khojas, and Pathans. Race and ethnic background were related to individual characteristics. Statements like "All Bengalis are cheaters" or "Sindhis are lazy" were not unusual. However, since honest Bengalis and hardworking Sindhis were easy to find, it was equally clear that these were not exceptionless generalizations. By the time I had left for North America, my education and experience had made me a staunch liberal. I believed that ultimately each individual deserved to be judged by what he or she did, and not by race affiliation. However, people know what stereotypes are applied to "their kind," and there is generally a grain of truth to every generalization, even though generalizations sometimes persist long after the truth has evaporated.

It was clear to me that race was a dimension to be reckoned with, even in supposedly egalitarian and fair-minded North America. Racism had been institutionalized by the enslavement of blacks, and the formal end of slavery had left deep social scars. In fundamental terms, a black could be bought and sold, whereas a white man could not. This set the races apart. The predominantly white students at Columbia had certain beliefs about blacks, based on decades of race-based division. Some of these beliefs were rooted in fear of retribution for slavery; a white boy was more likely to turn and run if he saw a big black man on a lonely Manhattan street than if he saw a white punk. However, I would have turned and run, too, since the street black was more likely to be poor, less vested in the system, and hence more violence-prone towards blacks and non-blacks alike.

Whites' beliefs about other non-white races were generally based on ignorance and broad stereotypes, since at that time there were few non-white communities in Manhattan other than Chinese, Puerto Ricans, and Cubans. Most non-whites belonged to the lower social classes. Through eradication of the American Indian, it seemed that Euro-American settlers had assertively acquired now the right to be top dog. America was "discovered" by Christopher Columbus, I was told; presumably, it did not exist before then. Non-whites were welcome in a genial, expansive, good-humored and liberal sort of way, as long as they played by the rules, knew their place, and did not get uppity. This applied as well to women, who were expected to grow up to become good wives. People from the Middle East, and those of other religions, such as Muslims and Buddhists, were small enough in number to be interesting trophies to be collected socially by progressive intellectuals at wine-and-cheese events.

As a foreigner who was expected to go home when he had finished his academic program, I was an "adopted white," a curiosity who was always welcome, and a source of learning about the world beyond the oceans. Race relations seemed to revolve around black and white, and, as a foreigner, I was neither. However, while I could beg off from allegiance to either camp while a visitor, it was clear that I was not of the privileged color, white. However, it was not clear at that point whether this was a disadvantage or an advantage.

The decade of the seventies was also a period that saw the Black Power and women's movements come of age. The Black Panthers, Stokely Carmichael, Malcolm X (in his posthumously published autobiography), and James Baldwin all spoke about race as the defining characteristic in white America. Kate Millett and other were launching the women's liberation movement, and co-ed dormitories and bra-less co-eds were "in." I was an active spectator to all these great social changes, including the birth of gay liberation. I attended anti-Vietnam talks at Columbia by Noam Chomsky, listened to Andrea Dworkin talk of female oppression, and watched silently as brave men surfaced to announce that they were gay. Through all this, my own race never arose as an issue. Perhaps it was an issue that I chose not to confront. More likely, if I was discriminated against because of race, I simply did not sense it, since I was always in fairly good control of my environment, and never underprivileged or dispossessed.

I have been occasionally asked about my experience with racism in America, and it is with some discomfort that I have had to confess that I have not felt particularly discriminated against. When I walk into a room of white men I know immediately that I am in the racial minority. This is not uncomfortable, in and of itself, since it is factually correct. However, I have also found that race is only point of discrimination. Other less, superficial forms, such as discrimination on the basis of class, culture and education, are often more potent. Perhaps I am simply insensitive to the racism directed at me. I concede that I may have some deep-seated mental blocks on this subject, which I have yet to uncover. Be that as it may, I find that concept of beauty, consumerism, discrimination against gays, and stratification by social class are just as difficult for me to deal with as how some deal with race. I have sometimes felt singled out for attention, or inattention, at events where I was the only non-white. This is similar to the attention given to whites or other foreigners who visited Pakistan. It is largely hospitable curiosity. I have rarely detected hostility behind the attention, particularly after I have joined the discussion at hand. This has not been true in public places; once, when entering an exclusive supermarket in an upscale neighborhood in the South that was effectively "whites only," I felt the stares of customers and employees alike. I was uncomfortable for a few moments, and then ignored this attention and went about my business. As non-whites gain a bigger share of power and wealth in North America, this imbalance will shift. In the interim, there will always be crazed rednecks who will act in response to their stereotypes and fears, and traditional corporate chiefs who will abdicate their leadership responsibilities and cater to their biases and to the superstitions of their employees. During this interim, minorities will pay the price for being non-white; they will be physically attacked, promoted more slowly or not at all, vilified, and marginalized.

Many whites in North America take personal credit for the achievements of their ancestors and, more broadly, the achievements of everyone white. This is as silly as my taking credit for the achievements of every Muslim or every Pakistani. However, empowerment through racial affiliation is being slowly eroded. It is difficult indeed to cede unearned power to those more deserving. The overpaid white union-man is seeing his job exported abroad or relocated to the black sweatshops of the American South, or to the Chinese sweatshops on the West Coast. The cozy, collegiate, upper-class, white, ivy-league establishmentarians are being invaded, and the more incompetent among them fired. It is curious to hear the whining among "conservatives" about affirmative action for blacks: preference in admission because of group affiliation has always been standard operating procedure among most business and academic institutions. If your father attended Harvard, or your uncle runs an investment bank, you are more likely to get admitted or get a job, irrespective of academic merit or competence.

In my view, being gay is a more important factor in being discriminated against than being non-white, unless one is an Afro-

American. In my relationships with Afro-Americans, I have striven to understand the deep sense of alienation, isolation, and rootlessness that sets them apart from the rest of the community. One enduring legacy of slavery is the extraordinary work required for Afro-Americans to fashion individual and group identities. The white mainstream marks them as inferior from birth because of race, and this presumptive label requires a lifetime of labor to erase. Unsurprisingly, few are able to achieve the stature that enables them to get beyond their natural bitterness at this handicap.

Stories abound of successful blacks who still cannot shake off race-based identification. In one story, the black chief executive officer of a major firm was mistaken for a valet by a white woman, who asked him to fetch her car. In another story, a black senior partner in a law firm was working in his office on a Saturday afternoon and was interrogated by a newly hired white lawyer about what he was doing in the office. These true stories illustrate how impossible it is to reposition social roles within a single generation. Curiously, I do not find the baggage of such discrimination to be carried by non-American blacks, such as those that are foreign born and have chosen to come to North America of their own free will. They are generally less troubled by whatever racism they encounter, and more able to shrug it off as a quirk and move forward with their lives. This is not "denial," it is common sense and survival. Clearly, there is much more to identity than skin color. American Jews excel in such pragmatic accommodation: many anglicized their names at the Ellis Island port of entry, and some, later, to be able to "pass" as non-Jew and avoid discrimination. Rather than fight a losing frontal battle against prejudice and ignorance, their focus on hard work and family has made them the model minority in the United States today, barely visible, quietly successful.

Greek Discoveries

It was a cold summer in the Greek islands. I was on vacation during a summer at college, on a ferry boat from Rhodes to Mykonos in the middle of the night. The pitch-black seas were rough, tossing the boat up and dropping it, then jerking it from side to side. The Greeks among us were curled up inside the cabin for the eight-hour voyage, impassively resigned to a bad, but necessary, journey. The tourists on board were milling about, joking about the bad weather or throwing up. The stench of fresh vomit filled the large common cabin, and people who had considerately gone to the deck to vomit had succeeded only in making it slippery with their bile. As I stood huddled in one of the corners, I could see a pathetic Greek woman whose two little children seemed to be throwing up all over their clothes. Nearby, a Canadian family loudly lamented about their trip to Greece so far. An observer in the corner, I surveyed the scene with some detachment and a stomach of iron, thinking, "At least it is warm."

We finally moored at Mykonos, at 3:00 A.M. The half-moon cast a pallor over the whitewashed houses that are the hallmark of Greek islands. After we landed on the jetty, the disembarking crowd frantically looked around. There was no one to receive us! Customarily, visitors are greeted by locals who rent rooms. The passengers milled around, many desperate about what to do. I stood there, traveling bag in hand, looking at the sleeping village, wondering whether to walk there or wait until someone showed.

A flash of baby blue caught my eye. It was his shirt, unbuttoned to the navel. The approaching man, wearing white pants and a wide Greek face, stopped and surveyed the milling crowed.

I moved towards him, as did the Canadian family.

He beckoned to me. "You need a room?" he asked.

"Yes!" I replied.

"Follow me."

Relieved, I followed him through the maze of passageways that are the streets of Mykonos, then into a small house. I followed him up the steep stairs. He introduced himself as Nikos, and then introduced his friend, Theo, who also appeared to be Greek. Introductions were performed in broken English. I smiled, we all laughed, and I told him that I was weary, ready to sleep. Nikos showed me to a bed in the adjacent room and then left.

I stripped and, as I got into bed, Theo entered the room and joined me and, without much more than a smiling glance, started to caress my crotch, while making playful cooing sounds. This was more of an invitation, rather than an aggressive sexual attack. Yet he obviously assumed that I would not object to pleasure, or that I was too tired to protest. He was right on both counts. Soon, he had my cock in his mouth and before long had completed the job. Spent and exhausted, I mumbled thanks and turned over to sleep.

It must have been shortly thereafter that I was awakened by the movement of another body next to mine. It was Nikos. He clasped me in his arms, but his hand soon dropped below my waist. Now it was his turn, he seemed to explain, in body language.

My droopy penis readied for an encore, while I felt his mouth envelop it. As I turned towards him to facilitate access to his mouth, he surprised me by turning around. He was naked, and his legs were open. He guided my erection into his cavity, his warm pudenda, his pre-lubricated hole. In a flash, my erection was buried inside his body, and he was arching his back, in total control. My hands crossed over his chest, caressed his smooth chest and taut nipples, and then moved down to his throbbing erection. My fingers probed behind his balls, where my body connected with his. My thrusts were instinctive and fluid, as though I had prepared for this moment all my life.

As I moved within him, I could feel his body's feedback, the squirming sounds of his satisfaction and the demands of his body as it moved in rhythm. As the pace of my thrusts quickened, I felt his sphincter muscles clamp down on me, as if to slow me down. Now fully awake, I rolled my body over his and seized control. His back pressed against my chest, the clammy skin of my loins slapped against his buttocks with each of my increasingly uncontrolled thrusts. His low moans and fitful body movements as he stroked himself further heightened the frenzy. Half conscious and quite exhausted, I seemed almost to be going through motions naturally, my eyes closed and this body in my arms, a high degree of sexual tension driving my thrusts. It was almost surreal, an erotic dream. Soon I burst within him. Exhausted, I pulled out to discover that he, too, had cum. Now spent, I collapsed over him, my still-tumescent penis inside him; we were both bathed in the aroma of his cum. I opened my eyes, as if suddenly awakened from the autopilot of sexual congress. Somewhat dazed by what had happened, I pulled out, jumped out of bed, and rushed to the toilet to wash myself clean.

When I returned, I noticed that Nikos had returned to his room, and that my bed was empty. However, he had thoughtfully put a little towel over the wet patch on the bed sheets where his semen had spurted. But I was too tired to think about what had just happened, and returned to sleep. I had been "deflowered" on the Greek Islands. What, in retrospect, could be more romantic?

The following morning Nikos, Theo, and I had a leisurely breakfast by the beach amidst whooping cranes and fishermen. He and his friend lived in London, where they were students, and this was a family vacation home. What had happened the night before was not discussed, and there was a casual intimacy in their demeanor that made me uncomfortable. They suggested we meet in London on my next trip. We talked about Greece, Europe, and Canada, which both had visited. I felt confused about the relationship that had developed between the three of us. Rather than secretive sex dismissed the morning after, it seemed almost as though this could develop into a social relationship, and I was unsure of how to proceed, and afraid to allow them to take the lead. I yearned for what they appeared to be offering, an invitation to join them in friendship, solidified rather than destroyed by our intimacy together.

Nikos and Theo were both "straight" in appearance. If I had met either in different circumstances, I could easily have introduced them to other friends. They were quite natural in their behavior, "normal" in every way, and appeared totally unaffected by the events of the night before. The problem was clearly mine. While I did not feel regretful or "guilty" about what had happened, I could not connect it with routine social interaction. These were two distinct worlds—the sexual and social—and I was tense and uncomfortable as we sipped strong Greek coffee and ate sweet yogurt and fruit on a perfect morning in Mykonos. They invited me to stay a few days longer, but I insisted I had to leave that day. I was running away from what I wanted.

That dreamy night with Nikos had also been my introduction to the "Greek way." I had found great pleasure being anchored within a man's body. It had been delightful to feel in control, to feel him respond, to stroke his erection and pleasure his impaled body. The mouth and the anus were alternative orifices, each with its own allure; but though the skillful blow-job prolongs the pleasurable journey to orgasm, it is essentially a passive activity for the one "being blown." While in the backdoor, I found pleasure in enjoying the satisfaction of my partner and of having his pleasure in my control.

Am I Muslim?

Islamic societies are outwardly conservative and conformist. Pakistan was designed to be an Islamic nation, at least in name: it is officially the Islamic Republic of Pakistan. Pakistan was created when the Indian subcontinent was granted independence from British rule in 1947. The division between India and Pakistan is based on religion: Islam is central to the country and to the identity of its population.

The founder, Mohammed Ali Jinnah, was born on December 25, 1876, in Karachi, and came from a family of Gujarati Khoja Muslims. He went to England for his law degree, and built a successful legal practice in Bombay. He is generally credited with crafting Pakistan in negotiations with Nehru and Gandhi, as the British were pushed out of the subcontinent. Jinnah led a conventional upper-middle-class lifestyle, and reportedly enjoyed a good drink from time to time. Alcoholic beverages are, of course, forbidden to Muslims. He delivered his speeches in English, being better versed in this language than in his regional tongue of Gujarati, or Urdu. The movie *Gandhi* somewhat disparagingly depicts Jinnah as uptight and distant, which probably does injustice to the personal passion and drive that must have been behind his crusade to create Pakistan. He died at a relatively young age, shortly after his dream of Pakistan had become a reality.

His sister, Fatima, died in the 1970s. She spent her last years revered for her brother's role in creating the country, and even ran for prime minister of Pakistan. A spinster, she, too, lived in aristocratic style in a house in the center of Karachi, which is preserved to this day as a national monument. She spoke to visitors in English, and the subject of social conversation was more often than not her pet poodle, groomed and supine by her side as she received visitors. (Dogs are considered unclean under Islam and not suitable as indoor pets. A Muslim worshipper has to repeat ablutions prior to prayer if he or she is touched by a dog.)

These were clearly not typical Muslims to have created and led a Muslim country. Indeed, the original vision was for Pakistan to be democratic and secular. However, they were typical of the "brown English" elite who had put into place the basic infrastructure of the new country of Pakistan and guided it for three decades. Though nominally Muslim, this generation was operationally unconcerned with the details of Islam. Many may have been privately religious, but they did not seek to impose the rituals and conventions of their interpretation on others. Rather, they sought to lead by example. Jinnah articulated a liberal vision for the country, grounded in the bureaucratic traditions of the British Civil Service, with tolerance for all religions.

Pakistan was created, in part, as a reaction to job and lifestyle discrimination against Muslims by the majority Hindus in pre-partition India. There was discontent across social classes. Pre-partition India was a hodgepodge of sects, religions, and languages, and the Hindu-Muslim divide was merely one such conflict. Basic differences in dietary habits and in religious beliefs contributed to contention. While these communal differences were generally kept under control, mutual hostility was often not far beneath the surface. The Muslim professional classes resented the second-class status for their community and seized the opportunity to push for a new Muslim-only country that would afford them the ability to run their own lives. Within the subcontinent, religion has long been a divisive issue, but often softened and without the rigid fundamentalist interpretations often common elsewhere. There are Hindus who eat meat and Muslims who drink alcohol. Perhaps this is partly because sectarian extremism was leveled somewhat by the British, which may also account for why not all Muslims chose to migrate to Pakistan after partition. The liberal tradition is hard to subdue. Even in the Muslim Mughal period, the arts were encouraged, and Mughal architectural accomplishments like the Taj Mahal stand to this day as testaments to that era of enlightened Muslim dominance of the subcontinent.

This liberal attitude was inherited by the elite that mobilized the subcontinent's Muslims to create Pakistan. The religions of Hinduism and Islam are, however, markedly different. Unlike Hindus, Muslims do not mark individuals at birth and place into a caste system from whence there is no escape. Islam rejects such birthright-based status, and as such Islam can be seen as a civilizing influence, empowering and unshackling individuals from the bonds of their past. Christianity played a similar role, and it is no surprise that most converts to Christianity in the subcontinent today are from the lower classes—society's outcasts. Islam also requires that Muslims respect those who believe in other religions, and the people around me in Pakistan took great pride in the fact that Hindu, Christian, Jewish, Parsi, and Buddhist minorities were not discriminated against.

That, at least, is the theory. While I recall no discrimination by members of my community against minority religions, in recent years I have spoken with Christians from Pakistan who recall being treated like second-class citizens while growing up. However, I have yet to encounter a non-Muslim from the Pakistan of my childhood who felt persecuted. My recollection, therefore, is of a tolerant and fair society. Since I was privileged, this probably limited my exposure to those who were biased, and so my observations are probably not authoritative.

I was raised a Muslim. I was born into a Muslim family in a country that is over ninety-eight percent Muslim. Everything about daily life was Muslim. It seemed that even the climate we lived in was Muslim. Islamic prescriptions and guidelines were often discussed in my house during my childhood, and there was frequent commentary and debate about its various tenets. Visitors, relatives, and my parents would sometimes bring up Quranic interpretations of various things, and there was often a lively difference of opinion. Islam was a living thing, a set of rules and regulations that was far more relevant than, for example, the central government. We were taught the Muslim view of the world. This view was applied to issues that included the role of women, the need for charity, issues of social justice, and the role of scientific inquiry and its conflict with belief. We would even question God's existence and nature, and debate the genesis of other religions. I learned of the great divide between religions "of the book" versus the religions of "idol worshippers." The Holy Quran recounts the stories of the Bible, and Islam accepts the prophets of Judaism and Christianity, the religions of the book. Islam accepts these as legitimate religions with connections to the same God, and Muslims are permitted to marry Christians and Jews. Hinduism, Zoroastrianism, Buddhism, animism and other religions are regarded as the inferior religions of idol worshippers, who thereby become candidates for conversion. A Hindu who marries a Muslim is therefore required to convert, as a prerequisite, while a Christian or a Jew is not. Growing up, I learned that Islam is more than a religion, but a way of life. Indeed, the Quran establishes laws, spells out rituals in some detail and, when coupled with the *Hadith*,[1] establishes a comprehensive set of conventions for an orderly society. Secular laws are subordinate to Quranic laws. The Quran is prescriptive on a wide variety of issues, and this sometimes raises practical problems. For example, the practice of lending money for interest is forbidden, but equity investment is not. I know Muslims who actively invest in the stock market, but refuse to accept interest on their bank accounts.

The actual practice of the rituals of Islam was often overlooked in our household, in favor of a more philosophical acceptance of its basic teachings. Islam requires prayer five times a day, but nobody in my family, except my mother and grandparents, did so regularly. My father occasionally found the time to pray privately or to visit the mosque for the communal Friday prayers and, when he did, we would sometimes go together as a family. Of course, we were all required to learn the Arabic prayers, and to read the Quran *Shareef* in Arabic.

We did, however, attend *Eid*[2] prayers regularly, after which we would entertain visitors and tally our gifts, typically

---

[1] The *Hadith* describes how Muhammad, the Prophet of Islam, lived life. It includes incidents, conventions, and rules. While it is not required that all Muslims follow this example, Muhammad's life is seen as worthy of emulation.

[2] *Eid* is celebrated twice each year, once to commemorate the end of a thirty-day fasting period, and once to celebrate the story of Abraham and Issac, when God substituted a goat for Abraham's son. The latter, known as *Bakr-Eid* (*bakra* means goat), requires that a goat be sacrificed and meat distributed

(*continued* . . .)

Edhi[1] money. We would wear new clothes and spend the day eating sweets and meeting relatives. Often we would visit the graves of ancestors and pray. These rituals were a normal part of being a Muslim in Pakistan. What it meant to be a Muslim was therefore deeply etched into my conscious and subconscious, even as I read books that described other religions and works by philosophers and theorists, such as Bertrand Russell and George Bernard Shaw, who mocked organized religion. I agreed intellectually with their view of religion as an opiate of the masses and took pleasure in proclaiming myself to be a freethinker. However, such intellectual masturbation rarely affected or influenced my acceptance of ritual and practice, nor did it have any real relevance to how I lived my life. As an intellectual dilettante, I found plenty to debate, but such talk was largely empty, and nothing that was proposed had the potential for real social impact, not even discussions of atheism and agnosticism. Even my occasional rejection of Islam in argument was accommodated within the religion. It was seen as the amusing intellectual gyrations of an adolescent.

In this regard, the Islam of my childhood was a remarkably tolerant and forgiving religion, a fact that may be surprising to the reader. Islam is portrayed as an extremist, severe, sinister, and harsh religion of little joy and even less freedom. There also seems to be a campaign of misinformation about Islam in the Christian West, sustained by the evidence provided by extremist fundamentalist factions that have emerged in some Muslim countries. Their actions permit Islam to be portrayed as a religion of

(... *continued*) ─────────────────────────────

to the poor. I would watch two servants hold down the animal, as one slit its throat with a sharp knife. Blood would spurt as the flailing animal slowly died. Typically, the meat was sent off to the local mosque, and the warm blood fertilized the rose bushes in the garden.

[1] On *Eid*, children are typically given small amounts of money as gifts.

intolerance and bigotry. I am not a scholar of Islam, but I believe that this is far from the truth.

In my understanding Islam is, in fact, a simple and democratic faith. It starts with fundamental assumptions, which must be axiomatically accepted as unquestioned truths. These beliefs include faith in one God and in his prophet Muhammad. Beyond these basic beliefs, the religion sets out basic rules that are little different from those of Christianity and Judaism, both of which are seen as legitimate forerunners to Islam. Islam seems more modern, however, with no organized hierarchy of priests or rabbis established to intercede or interpret direct communication between man and God.

Faith is also a communal event. Thus, Friday prayers are an occasion for the community to get together and socialize, for the *maulavi*[1] to sermonize and to lead the group prayers. Prayers are recited in Arabic, and all Muslims are urged to study Arabic to understand what is said. The commentary following the prayer ritual, with its precise sequence, is in the native language, which is Urdu in Karachi. Within this communal framework, questions are raised in an open forum and debated. There is no social penalty for voicing dissent, as long as it is in the spirit of learning the right answer, which, if contained in the Quran, and debated. This exercise of freedom within Quranic constraints is intended in Muslim society to promote debate and discussion, virtuous behavior, and charity. Equality and egalitarianism are at the heart of Islam. It is said that the great Caliph Haroon Rasheed would disguise himself as a peasant and mingle with the

---

[1] The *maulavi*, or *maulana*, is a man who devotes himself to understanding the Quran. He is respected for his dedication and effort, but occupies no formal position, though he may be associated with organizational activities related to running a mosque.

people, in order to understand their needs directly. I was taught that the heroes of Islam are those who seek justice and are humble in the privileged positions they may occupy, and that no such position is unattainable by any other Muslim. In this sense, Islam embodies modern democratic ideals, within the community of Muslims.

I intellectually rejected religion and the literal definitions of God, heaven, and hell at a fairly young age. It was apparent to me that the various paradoxes associated with the balance between omnipotence and free will could simply not be resolved. It was also apparent to me that it was entirely possible to lead a "good" life without believing in a literal interpretation. While religion was good—indeed, essential—for society in general, I could do quite nicely without it for myself. I am nominally "Muslim," though I see it now more as a cultural affiliation than as a belief system. If I were to seriously select a religion, though, it would be Islam.

Islam permits multiple wives (up to four) for each man, but there are strict requirements for fairness and equity for each wife in such an arrangement. These requirements include financial and emotional parity, and implicitly include regular sexual congress, which is considered a natural and normal requirement for healthy adults. Operationally, most men I knew had neither the financial wherewithal nor the stamina to marry more than one woman.

Marriage is also a business contract, duly signed and witnessed. The wife and husband each enter into this contract to raise a family and to become part of the community. When married, a man becomes an adult and a full community member. Islamic property laws are also remarkably protective of the rights of women. Property does not automatically get commingled or change hands through marriage, except as contractually agreed. For example, a woman may bring along a dowry.[1] A man is required to commit to a *huq mehr*[2] at the time of marriage, the amount to reflect his financial station in life. A wife can demand this in settlement at will, and it is designed to protect her with a financial cushion should she choose to leave her husband. While the dowry is intended to become part of the household, a woman's property remains hers should the union be dissolved. This seems to me to be a remarkably civilized way to protect the legal rights of women.

Regarding its treatment of women, Islam appears to me to be remarkably even-handed and pragmatic, in comparison with other major religions at the time of its rise. I have heard of a Jewish prayer that starts: "Thank God for not making me a woman . . .", thereby making a clear statement about male superiority. While not an expert in comparative religion, the asexual confusion of Christianity in the Virgin Birth of Jesus, and the self-immolation expected by Hindu women on their husbands funeral pyre, are similarly concepts that are strange to me. Islam demands strength from women, in the home and in the outside world. Muslim businesswomen and property owners are not uncommon, difficult perhaps to believe for readers that associate Islam with the veil and female subservience. Keep in mind that the Islam practiced in some of today's culturally primitive societies is materially different from the prescribed religion.

Islam is also designed to be relatively guilt-free for believers. Unlike the Catholic notion of sin, repentance, and forgiveness

---

[1] The dowry becomes part of the household, but its ownership is retained by the woman.

[2] This is a sum of money written into the marriage contract. The woman may choose to leave her husband at any time, and he is legally required to give her this money on demand. It protects her against, for example, an abusive husband.

by a priest at confession, Islam is directly prescriptive where worldly crimes are concerned, and the Islamic notion of justice is swift, and can be extreme (such as, chopping off a hand for theft). Where there are offenses that cannot be directly punished, accountability is deferred until after death. Irrespective, redemption is through action rather than pious retreat.

This pragmatic approach is directly relevant to the way Islam handles issues related to sex and sexuality. The search for responsible pleasure is not fettered; however, responsibility is well defined and directly references the contractual family unit. Thus, a married man who is traveling away from his family for extended periods may seek the solace of concubines, or a man whose wife is infertile may take a second wife in order to breed. A man with a sexual appetite more voracious than his wife can accommodate may seek consorts. However, in all these cases no shame must come to the family, making discretion essential. In keeping with the spirit of responsibility, a man is responsible for the financial support of any children he fathers. Note that while polygamy is permitted, polyandry is not. This again reflects the marriage contract: if a man is expected to support his children, then he must be unambiguously certain that the children are his. Given today's reality of birth control and DNA testing, should these rules be adjusted?

In this framework, sex between men is a non-issue, as long as it does not affect marriage and is kept as a private matter. In fact, as Persian poets and Islamic mystics have described it, the love of boys can be a very noble and uplifting thing. As two separate events, a mystic may sacrifice inclusion in society and also take on a male lover. In some sense, he then taps into the spiritual dimension of Islam, and goes beyond the practical to the more mystical aspects of God.

In Pakistani society, *Gandus*[1] are derided because they are seen as lustful and because lust *per se* is thought to be surrender to an appetite, which is considered harmful, since it saps resolve and undermines social responsibility. Sex with a wife is a step towards breeding and is therefore wholesome and desirable. Note that remarriage after divorce is permitted for both women and men; Islam does not deny women sexual satisfaction or the companionship of a husband, nor does it seek to rob sex of its natural attribute of pleasure.

The notion of choosing between being homosexual and being Muslim therefore never occurred to me. I felt completely natural as I was. I felt no guilt about my sexual desire for men. No one said it was wrong. All my sex partners were either married or expected to marry. I, too, always expected to marry one day; marriage was never to be seen as an alternative to sex with a man, but as a social supplement. Romantic love is not needed or expected in order to make a successful marriage. I realized implicitly from the start that such an arrangement would be necessary for me as well. Since I fully expected to be able to acquit myself honorably of the responsibilities associated with marriage, I perceived no need to disclose my sexual interest in men to my family, nor to make it an issue in my relationship with a wife. I saw nothing devious, dishonest, or dishonorable about this.

Asserting that one is gay is a political act. It elevates homosexuality to social identity. As such, it sets up the possibility of a social union based solely on a romantic connection, a union with a goal other than reproduction of a family. This is where the conflict between being gay and Muslim arises. It is also the reason "coming out" is so difficult and somewhat meaningless for a

---

[1] *Gandu* is a perjorative for a passive male partner.

Muslim, even though there may be no reluctance to engage in homosexual acts, or even to enter into loving same-sex relationships. Coming out implies that a man is rejecting his social and family responsibilities, which is tantamount to dropping out. And, in Muslim societies, to drop out is to disappear. There is nowhere to go, since everyone else is family-defined. The absence of love is a small price to pay for social survival. Only a man foolhardy enough to go crazy with love would attempt this, and folk stories like *Laila Majnu* (closely parallel to Romeo and Juliet) attest that love and romance are alive and well in Pakistani folklore.

Talking about who one has sex with is gratuitous vulgarity. Therefore, for a man who feels romantically towards another man, there is really nothing to say to anybody else. The two men cannot even run away and threaten to create a family unit. In fact, they would not need to flee as long as personal desire is kept discreetly separate from social obligation. Unless they choose to raise a fuss, their desires do not matter.

Return of the Expatriate

*M*y first year at Columbia was exciting. I was on a fast learning curve. Everything was new, but the rules that applied were easy to understand. There was a clear structure and easily identified logic to all procedures, social and academic. Rules were written, requirements were defined, and consequences were predictable. My American fellow freshmen were themselves lonely from being away from home, often for the first time, and their nervousness and anxiety was easy to diagnose and relate to.

During this year I was an eager student of the American psyche. The concerns of my fellow students were so different from my previous concerns: the threat of nuclear war, where to eat, and how to waste time with group leisure activities, such as bridge. Most of my cohorts were American, but there was a significant contingent of foreigners, with whom I developed a natural affinity. Unlike many of these students, however, my feelings did not include any sort of sentimental yearning to return to the community I had come from. What we had in common was a feeling of being disconnected from our pasts in this different cultural environment. I found it a great challenge, and tremendous fun, to sharpen my skills at discussion, at arguing and questioning the assumptions that were the basis for what was around me.

There was very little sexual discussion, and most of the undergraduates around me did not have girlfriends. There was light banter about the need to pick up girls at the various mixers that were held, but there was no peer pressure to "score" by taking a girl to bed. This was generally a serious group focused on academics, although some of the boys had steady girlfriends who occasionally stayed over in their dormitory rooms.

I missed the familiarity of family, and traveled back to Pakistan from time to time to visit. During these trips, I met other Pakistanis who had gone to study abroad in countries ranging from England to Australia. There was a community of expatriates in my age range who shuttled back and forth between Karachi and various international destinations. We got to know each other fairly well, to compare our lives and experiences, and to discuss academic programs and plans.

Paki-Bonding

One of these friends, Aurangzeb, was from Karachi. He and I grew to become close friends, in part because he had an intellectual's openness to all subjects. We often discussed the nature of life and relationships. He enjoyed the arts and literature. He dressed well, had a sense of style and the commanding presence of a dandy. Unlike with my other Pakistani friends, we did not dwell on the common conventions of our social backgrounds. Through unspoken mutual consent we avoided discussion, except in abstract terms, of the inevitability of marriage, women, or differences in the backgrounds of our families, and this established a comfort zone between us. These were the subjects that isolated me from other Pakistanis I met at school; they would try to put me foremost in social context, and inevitably my response to their inquisitiveness would be defensive or protective, reserved and distancing. Aurangzeb, however, was outspoken in his personal views about freedom from convention and the need to be creative. He had an outgoing, attractive personality and quickly developed friendships with people he met. We discussed the works of Jean Genet and Gore Vidal, who he agreed was the greatest living American writer (I had just read *The City and the Pillar*). Our tastes seemed similar, but our discussion and critical commentary of works such as these was always detached from our personal lives. However, I sensed within him a kindred soul. He spoke of principles and values, and seemed sensitive to my need for privacy. At the same time, he did not seem to be conventionally grounded. Like me, he appeared to be investigating his identity, taking tentative steps along unfamiliar terrain.

Aurangzeb was a student at Boston University. We were in the same freshman class—he, at BU and I, at Columbia. Eventually in his junior year, he transferred to Columbia and took up residence at an apartment just a few blocks from my dormitory. We would see each other from time to time, but since I lived at the dormitory and he was physically further away, our relationship consisted of sporadic meetings for dinner or an occasional art show or lecture. He appeared well settled in and was far more attuned to social happenings at the university than was I. When I wanted a break from my studies, I would call him to find out about local university events or social activities elsewhere in Manhattan. Usually I found that what he found interesting was also of interest to me. He was always on his way to a party and, when I joined him, I found his circle of friends to be attractive, opinionated, and fun to be with.

Concurrently I had also developed a close friendship with Pablo, a charming and articulate gay radical, with a swashbuckling style that was naturally warm and intimate. Pablo was from Puerto Rico and traced his lineage back to Madrid, Spain. He was a PH.D. student whose never-finished doctoral thesis was "to break new ground in cross-cultural explanations of homosexuality." Pablo was the most outspoken and naturally gay man I had ever met. He would pass comment on the shapes of men's bodies as we walked past, and rate them with humor and a wry turn of phrase. He would speak of his lust for the ones he liked and was ruthless in his witty put-downs of men who did not pass inspection. Pablo would speculate, after eyeing an attractive black man's crotch, about how well hung he was. He would gaze appreciatively at the all-American football types, as well as the petite Latinos. He was truly an equal-opportunity partner and enjoyed talking of his sexual exploits the night before. Pablo would frequent gay bars in Greenwich Village and then relate his encounters with me, vivid multisyllabic descriptions of lechery and lust. I enjoyed his company, since his adventures were always so much more interesting than mine. He was an exuberant slut, in the finest sense of the word. I learned more about lovemaking between men vicariously from Pablo than from any textbooks about homosexuality I had read—and well before I had my own experiences to draw upon.

Pablo viewed his attraction to men as the most natural thing in the world. He had told both his conservative, god-fearing Catholic parents that he was gay. After initial despair, they had accepted their son's inclinations with resignation. What they found more difficult to stomach was his open penchant for promiscuity and his delight at describing his sexual encounters, even in their presence. He had moved out of his family's home but did not neglect his filial duties. He would call his mother frequently and visit every Sunday for dinner.

Pablo was dangerous to anyone's closet. He had not a shred of discretion, not a whit of sensibility, not a scosh of delicacy. He was direct. So he definitely had to be kept far away from straight friends who were not to be told and, even more, from any fellow Pakistanis.

As fate would have had it, Aurangzeb met Pablo at a reading by Alan Ginsberg in the Village. They became instant friends. Before long, Pablo had ascertained that Aurangzeb fancied men. Moments later, my name had come up, and all the right connections had been made.

When I met Aurangzeb and he told me he had met Pablo at the poetry reading, my first instinct was to distance myself from Pablo. "Just a casual friend," I preemptively protested.

"Well," said Aurangzeb, "It seems that we all have a lot in common. . . ."

And the wall between us crumbled as he made it clear that Pablo had told him of my sexual encounters with men. Panic set in, as I realized that Aurangzeb knew my family, my friends—all about me that mattered. But then I realized that his position was as exposed as mine, and alarm gave way to reassurance. We started to talk, tentatively at first. Slowly, over the coming weeks, we started to share our experiences, devoid of the filter of normalcy that was reserved for the rest of the world.

Aurangzeb told me of men in Karachi who had sex with other men, how easy it was, and how prevalent. He talked of relationships he had had there, the male lovers who had passed through his life. He told me there were many happily married family men in Pakistan who had male lovers in the background.

He spoke contemptuously of gay bars in Manhattan and wistfully of the open-air pickup scene of Karachi.

Disbelieving, I listened to every word, challenging him at every step. What he was describing was incredible. How could I have grown up in the same city as he, yet been so oblivious to this undercurrent?

Aurangzeb took me to gay bars in Manhattan, but I found that my shy style was at odds with his extroverted cruising. Rather than get closer to him because of this shared secret, I found myself keeping him at a distance in Manhattan. Though he was as vulnerable to exposure as I, his bold and self-assured style scared me. We would meet and talk often, but I resisted his attempts to take me out at night. It would be almost a decade later, when he had moved to California and I was settled in Toronto, that we would finally meet in Karachi, and I would start to uncover directly the side of Karachi life he spoke about. Then a veil would lift, and the two-dimensional landscape of the Karachi of my youth would give way to a better-rounded world of sexuality and poetry, casual lust and deeply romantic relationships.

Diddling the Natives

I had taken several trips to Pakistan over a period of years before I got my first chance to test the truth behind the stories Aurangzeb had told me about Karachi.

"Karachi," he had declared "is a cesspool of lust."

He had spoken of sex parties with friends, of three-way sessions that included oral and anal intercourse (including one particularly delightful story about how he and another man simultaneously inserted their erect penises into the anus of a third man. "You come very quickly that way," he had confided).

Of course, Aurangzeb had been quick to agree when I pointed out that the privacy he enjoyed made this type of licentiousness possible. He lived in a large house with his parents. An only son, he had turned one of the wings of his parents' house into a private living area, an independent apartment. This apartment had a separate entrance, and its only access to the rest of the house was through a door that was usually locked. His tastefully furnished rooms were attended by a personal manservant. While he went to the main house for meals, much of his life was as independent as he wanted it to be. His parents were both very busy, so he had an extraordinary degree of freedom. His father was a wealthy industrialist and his mother a socialite.

Aurangzeb had to be careful to neutralize the network of servants in the main household, so that his privacy would be complete. His manservant, Bashir, was chosen independently, and did not have a prior social connection with the servants in his parents' house. Bashir was from a remote village in Sind and had migrated to Karachi for a job, to earn the money to return to his village and marry. The clearly established rules of his employment with Aurangzeb were included the requirement that he keep his distance from the adjacent household. The master paid well. The servant dutifully came in as required for the morning cleaning, cooked meals, was available as needed throughout the day, and then left after dinner. Aurangzeb had even arranged for living quarters for Bashir some distance away.

It could hardly escape Bashir's attention that young men would occasionally visit the house and that some would wander about almost naked, with just a towel to cover their loins. Bashir's job was to make breakfast, not to wonder and hold opinions. His master was kind and considerate, and he had no interest in passing judgment. Aurangzeb is unmarried and horny, Bashir might reasonably conclude, and being young and rich, why not have boys over for pleasure? As a servant in an influential household, he had to be discreet and uphold his master's family honor. This was just a job.

Aurangzeb was therefore able to blend a respectable life within his parent's house with the freedom he needed. He would pick up young men to bring over to his house and have sex with, and in fact had a regular "stable" that serviced him over time. There was turnover, as new men were added and older ones were abandoned or simply left town. Aurangzeb liked his men young and muscular, so he gravitated naturally toward men from the North, beautiful Pathans and *gandami*-skinned[1] Punjabis. He found plenty of men, lonely and available, horny and ready, sincere and warm with tenderness. It did not take much coaxing to get them back to his lair, with its soft music and firm bed.

While we were in Karachi together one summer, Aurangzeb took me cruising, Karachi style. He knew his turf well. As we drove along bustling streets, he outlined the basic rules for spotting someone looking to be picked up, which I was to follow by his example. He laid out various scenarios: the man would stand near a roundabout, where cars had to slow down; or an available man would stand on the side at a slow stretch of road, where there was space for a car to pull over.

"Notice," Aurangzeb would tell me, "how that young man there is standing slightly apart from the rest of a crowd? Look how he's dressed. Kind of nattily, but that scarf around his neck, a simple touch, is a giveaway that he'll offer sex for money."

---

[1] *Gandam* is wheat. A light wheat-colored complexion is considered highly desirable, whether in a woman or a man.

Or, indicating another young man on the street corner, Aurangzeb would lecture, "Now see that fine specimen there? He's dressed in clean, pressed clothes, so you might overlook him. But watch him. You see, he's got those alert eyes, like a hunter."

Aurangzeb drove by and caught the man's eyes. "And always, the special eye contact, like that, you know what I mean? It's like radar. We know exactly what each other has in mind."

However, as Aurangzeb pointed out, these regulars to the scene were not the only prey to hunt. Aurangzeb was also interested in "straight" men who could be seduced. Not only was the challenge keener, but there would be less of the affectation that he despised among those who were more readily available at street corners.

Aurangzeb brought considerable skill to the task of spotting an available sex partner and was able to quickly ascertain whether the stranger he had just met was suitable. Those who were not available and interesting would be quickly let out. He would pick up a Pathan worker on his way home, who had freshly showered at the end of the workday and was interested in discreet sex and companionship before rejoining his comrades. Or he would select a university student on his way home, who was ready to play. In fact, Aurangzeb maintained that any attractive man in Karachi could be had and would consent to having his clothes removed for at least body contact. If one wanted to be fucked, or to suck, the list of available young men approached one-hundred percent Any healthy man would welcome this release, he insisted. If one wanted to fuck, or to be sucked, then the available pool was smaller. This was limited to younger men who were readily intimidated or seduced into a new experience, men who were actually interested and readily willing, or to the semiprofessionals. Younger men, he explained, would find it easier to be fucked than to suck, since many had already been deflowered earlier by a horny male relative. This was particularly true, he maintained, of the Pathans and Baluchis, among whom strict tribal customs were still enforced and women were strictly segregated. If mutual masturbation, body contact, and frottage were the limited aim, then almost any good-looking young man would be available.

Aurangzeb also cheerfully explained that even if a man were not interested, his overtures could be readily laughed away without consequence. He would simply apologize and blame his erect penis for his forward behavior. If consummation was not fated, then the key was to devise an exit strategy that saved face for both parties.

One evening we were driving at night after dinner together, when he spotted a student walking by the side of the road. The young man, who appeared to be in his late teens, had clearly just missed his bus and was slowly walking home. This was not a man looking for a pickup.

"I will show you how," Aurangzeb said. "Just sit quietly and do not react."

Aurangzeb slowed the car and lowered the window. The youth came over. He was perhaps seventeen, with nascent wisps of a sturdy postpubescent mustache.

"Do you want a ride?" asked Aurangzeb.

"Sure."

Aurangzeb opened the back door and the young man hopped in, juggling his armload of books.

Aurangzeb made small talk: What was his name? *Ali.* Where did he live? *PIB Colony* (a lower middle-class neighborhood). Where did he study? He answered with the name of a nearby school.

I sat in the front seat, looking straight ahead. Keeping his right hand on the wheel, Aurangzeb reached over to the back seat, and I could tell that he was stroking the student's leg. He continued the friendly, interested patter, and the student's responses became increasingly strained. His voice broke, and he was clearly defocusing on the conversation. He was squirming; his tone was becoming more intense. From the corner of my eye, I could see Aurangzeb's arm movements, now rhythmic and regular. Finally, curiosity got the better of me.

I turned around to get a better look. The student's trousers were unbuttoned. His erect penis was in Aurangzeb's steadily pumping grip. His testicles were also visible, taut and tight under the shaft of his cock. The young man was clearly enjoying it. However, I had made a *faux pas*. As we made eye contact, he became uncomfortable. Though I turned around quickly, the magic had clearly been lost.

"Just drop me here," announced the young man, and despite Aurangzeb's continued sweet purring, he insisted. Aurangzeb stopped the car, and the young man got out, thanking him for the ride. I could see his still-hard cock, outlined under his now-buttoned pants.

"Why did you do that?" Aurangzeb exploded as we resumed driving. "I was getting him ready for you! If you had given me a few more minutes, you could have gotten in the back seat with him. He was almost ready!"

I had clearly made a tactical error and embarrassed the student into retreat. Aurangzeb, however, had demonstrated his finesse.

Creating A Safe Haven

During his university years in the United States, Aurangzeb spent his summers in Karachi. After completing his bachelor's degree, he returned to live in Karachi. His family was affluent and well established, and he could easily have purchased his own house. However, as an unmarried son, he was expected to continue to live with his parents. His family, friends, business associates, and others would have found it remarkable and a bit puzzling if he had chosen to move out without concurrent marriage plans. They would suspect a rift within the family as the only explanation. Aurangzeb had no real choice. He also had no good reason for a move, since he had ample freedom within the family structure.

Since he was still in his mid-twenties, Aurangzeb could reasonably argue that he was too young to marry just yet, that his stay in Pakistan was just a hiatus between undergraduate and graduate school, and he wanted to postpone building a family. This did not prevent family friends and relatives from proposing that he meet eligible girls. His closest friends and family, though, knew that he was definitely off the marriage market. More distant relatives, though, expressed their affection and family feeling for him by trying to help connect him with eligible girls. Since he was single, there was little else for them to talk with him about. This was the current bottleneck in his life plan, since he was educated and affluent. Later, after he married, his talk would turn to his children and their problems. I have seen unmarried men harassed by family and relatives for years, even when it was apparent that marriage was not on their minds. For the most part Aurangzeb won reprieve from the need to marry by proclaiming to his immediate family that he was not yet ready to settle down.

There was no question, however, that Aurangzeb's life plan in Pakistan would include marriage. Wedlock was not an option to be weighed, but a step forward in life that all men must take, to become socially independent, to extend and expand the family organism. Unmarried men are still extensions of their parents; it takes marriage and its commitments to define maturity. This is the social and religious custom in Pakistan, and no exceptions are allowed, except for well-documented and easily understood reasons, such as the need to care for an ailing parent, or a physical or mental disorder. A preference for sex with men could not be considered a valid reason for not getting married. Sexual desire is not a major reason for marriage. As long as the sexual equipment is functional, marriage is expected. Marriage is a responsibility to family, and not a personal indulgence. Marriage brings otherwise distant families together, and creates new families in the process. It enables renewal, focuses attention to the future, and creates a reason to live. Ultimately, it creates the promise of children, to delight in and enjoy, to pamper and spoil with overindulgence.

In a subsistence economy with limited recreational alternatives and few social options, children play a crucial role. In an abstract sense, they continue the bloodline. But children also evoke great protective tenderness and love and inspire social cohesion. It is expected that parents will sacrifice personal gratification for the sake of their children. Affluent parents pamper and spoil their children, with little of the concern for discipline that is typical in the West. I know of one family in which the mother did not leave her children alone a single moment, day or night, from their infancy until they went to school; her husband accepted this. In another instance a mother died prematurely, when her son was an infant; her sister married her husband to ensure that the child continued to receive familial care and not risk an unaffectionate stepmother. Children are given tremendous latitude to throw tantrums and are fussed over. The economy may be stagnant, there may be few creative arts or fine restaurants for entertainment, but the fresh and innocent perspective of children is sought to dispel the despair of daily life. Children are a joy to have around and symbolize life.

We all seek to become immortal in some small way. For royalty and old families, relevant acts are those that can create history, and even the reckless individual acts of monarchs are measured within the family context. But for most of us, living beyond today is reduced to saving for retirement, or writing a book to collect dust in library archives, or somehow making a mark. We often dull our iconoclastic humanity by feeding our senses with packaged entertainment, so that such questions do not arise and seem silly and contrived if they do. In a subsistence economy like Pakistan's, children represent a path to immortality; they provide wholesome, round-the-clock entertainment and a reason to live and strive. In this sense, they are the best deal around. This may also be true elsewhere, but in developed economies, children must compete for attention with a variety of forms of entertainment, and children are merely one of several avenues to immortality. This is particularly true for the large subset of children who grow up and reject their parents, thereby making those alternatives seem more credible. In Pakistan, there are no other options and, without children, life loses much of its meaning.

In Pakistani movies, even the most heinous crime is forgivable if committed by a mother to save her child. While conspicuous consumption and adult hedonism are generally disdained, pampering a child to excess is seen as nothing more than an expression of love. I have met adults who have lived with their parents all their lives and have yet to experience their first trauma of independence. In some ways, they are less self-sufficient than a high school student in North America.

It was thus seen as a sacrifice for Aurangzeb to delay his family-building for the sake of his planned graduate work. He let it also be known that he was helping his family by taking over an important and emerging part of the family business enterprise, so that his selflessness would be doubly admired. Relatives worried that he should perhaps find a wife now, to help him with his hard work. Some chided his mother for being too selfish to let him go.

This interim freedom gave Aurangzeb a rare opportunity to explore what Karachi had to offer. He had created an environment in which his hedonism could thrive, and buttressed it by keeping his family at arm's length to give himself space. He avoided extended-family gatherings whenever possible, to minimize the constant pressure to meet prospective brides. Rather than using his day to dwell on his identity and worry about the future family planned for him, Aurangzeb dedicated himself instead to having a good time.

Building and Managing a Stable

When I met Aurangzeb on a visit to Karachi a year after he had moved back, he referred to his "stable," and told me that he was having a wonderful time in Karachi.

"New York can have its Greenwich Village," he proclaimed. "Karachi is the place to be. This is the most wonderful environment to find real men. Those New Yorkers are all jaded sluts. I prefer my men to be innocent and affectionate, warm and real. I need love, and I have found it in so many ways in

Karachi, right in my backyard. I needed New York to awaken me, but this is the place to find men and to slake one's thirst!"

Aurangzeb had created for himself a cadre of regulars whom he contacted from time to time. These men, typically in their early twenties, served his need for companionship and sex in different ways. Some were purely sexual partners, picked up for their instant sex appeal. There was a high turnover in this group. Others had more to offer, and he was able to talk with them, to blend sex with friendship. He would meet them from time to time, discuss their troubles, and advise them about their problems. Occasionally he would help them get jobs or find housing, and in return they would do favors he requested, such as run errands to find a special new Hollywood movie that he had heard was now available on video. He could trust these men, and they knew where he lived and who he was. They were in some sense his gay social family, but because they were separated by class, they could not aspire to get any closer. These relationships evolved into easy and familiar intimacy, with the unstated understanding of limits. There were few expectations in these simple relationships, and they were ultimately sustained to assuage loneliness and for mutual benefit. They could be terminated by either party without explanation, or suspended for extended periods of time. Other obligations took precedence; the man could go back to his village to get married, or Aurangzeb could decide that he was too busy to see him. Aurangzeb was a *seth*—a rich man—in their eyes, and they could hardly expect him to surrender his freedom or flexibility for them. Rather, they were grateful to have attracted his sustained interest, and he was generous with his attention when he was with them. There were few hard feelings.

Each of these men knew that there were other men that Aurangzeb consorted with. They knew without asking that they had no exclusive right to Aurangzeb, and they had no expectations in this regard. The only exclusive relationships in Karachi are those based on family connection, those that network parents and children. These relationships are private and sacrosanct. All other relationships are temporary. Even deep friendships, sustained through mutual interest and the work needed to maintain the link, can disintegrate over time. Family, however, endures even in the absence of effort, and bloodlines persist and are unseverable.

Meeting new people, Aurangzeb explained, was easy. For casual sex partners, he would simply drive late at night and pick up a suitable candidate. A typically illiterate Pathan, far away from home and lonely, with a giant erection and a soft touch would do quite nicely. Frequently such men had their own solitary work lives to deal with. In some cases, periodic sexual contacts would continue over an extended period of time. Aurangzeb liked variety. He liked the simple love these men had to offer, their tenderness, and lack of expectations.

Once he felt comfortable with a man, Aurangzeb would have no compunction about taking him to his room for sex. He had little fear of being blackmailed. Such an attempt would not be taken seriously by family and friends; a more significant concern was the prospect of a violent altercation or theft. Sex with another man is technically illegal (anal sex still carries with it a maximum penalty of ten year's hard labor—a legal legacy from British common law), but being accused of doing it would be laughed at.

"You can go now," he would tell his servant, then lock the doors and proceed to have his way.

The Saga Of Haider

Aurangzeb also taught me that Karachi offered a variety of possible relationships. At one meeting after a six-month break in communication, he proclaimed to me that he was three months into a "real" relationship with an engineering student. This young man was twenty-one years old, and he had picked him up on Zebunnisa Road at the Pak-American bookstore. His striking good looks and large, regal nose had attracted Aurangzeb for some reason, but it was his sensual lips and the open invitation in his eyes that had finally established a connection. It had been midday, but Aurangzeb took Haider to his room for a quick fuck. This could have been risky, since he did not yet know the boy well. However, he instinctively felt comfortable with him.

"He took off his clothes and lay on his belly," recounted Aurangzeb. "He wanted me to fuck him, without preliminaries, you know what I mean? His last lover had used him like a piece of meat. I could see why. His naked body is beautiful, and, believe me, just the sight of his smooth buttocks gave me an instant erection. He was Sindhi, like me, but he was well muscled and took care of his body, unlike so many Sindhis.

"As I was entering him, he just lay there, but once I was inside him, he really came to life. He thrashed around, moaning and groaning passionately while I fucked him. And, oh!, that sphincter of his gripped me so tightly. I had an unbelievably great orgasm. And he is so well hung and insisted on jerking off without any help from me—it was such a pity, but I so enjoy watching him satisfy himself, if you know what I mean. He is so hot. . . . Each session of sex with him is like the last one of his life . . . he puts his entire mind and body into the here and now. . . . When we're through, I have to clean the room and put things back into place—we fuck in the bed, on the floor, everywhere."

Aurangzeb paused, momentarily lost in a private thought, then continued: "Anyway, when I first met him he had an intense, sad look in his eyes, and I knew from the start he was suffering under some problem. For some reason . . . I have become quite attached to him, you know what I mean? . . . We have been seeing each other quite regularly since we first met.

"One thing has changed, gradually. He's sucking me! You know, I so enjoy sucking him, and I have taught him that it is not unmanly to suck! That was quite a breakthrough! Now we have foreplay. He is quite amazing. I can drive him into a wild state, and he can cum several times in a single session of lovemaking. His cum has a nice salty flavor, like *lassi*,[1] you know what I mean? So sex is great."

His eyes, which had just flashed with so much excitement, now turned sad. "However, his family is *dihati*[2] and want him to get married even though he is just twenty-one. They have even found a girl for him from their village near Hyderabad; she is just twelve, but such things are no surprise to you. He has been making excuses, of course, but he's running out of them. He gets his college degree in three months. Well, the poor lad has even talked of suicide, so I have to deal with both passion and pain each time I see him!

"I don't know what to do. Haider seems to have become attached to me, and I must confess that I have also become quite close to him. Of course, I still see the others in my stable from time to time just for sex, you know what I mean? But Haider—he is in a different category. . . . I must admit that I'm

---

[1] A fermented milk drink.
[2] Villagers.

somewhat afraid of him, of his passion and his need. He feels so trapped. In a different setting, I could easily fall in love with him. What can I do?"

He paused again, his forehead furrowed as he pondered his dilemma. Then he shook his head as if he'd just agreed with a thought his mind proffered. "He cannot survive here, and I cannot continue this relationship, much as I would want to." He shrugged, laughing, "I am drowning in too much love and sex, you know what I mean?"

I met Haider one day at Aurangzeb's house, and the change in Aurangzeb was striking when he was with the young man. The suave and polished New Yorker in him had dissolved into mush around Haider. Aurangzeb fawned over Haider, and worried with him about little things. He gave him a new shirt. He asked about his job and gave him advice. He offered him things to eat and chided him for not taking better care of his health. It was clear that Haider had pierced the armor of Aurangzeb's heart.

Haider was about five feet, eleven inches tall, slightly taller than Aurangzeb. He had thick, dark-brown hair, which was neatly combed over his broad, smooth forehead. His eyes were a deep and expressive black, perched astride a broad nose, under which was a wispy mustache, visibly darker than his head of hair. His full sensuous lips stretched easily into a smile. His angular chin was bare, and his naked throat was disproportionately thin and delicate, with a knobby Adam's apple that bobbed up and down when he was nervous. Haider had a warm and affectionate gaze, which could transform instantly into a carnal look, such as when he turned towards Aurangzeb. With the charm and guile of youth, he was naturally seductive.

Whatever the nature of the love between them, there was clearly no monogamy required of Aurangzeb, who would continue to cruise from time to time, to nourish and supplement his stable with new men. One of these men was a helper at the squash courts at the Karachi Club. One day before dinner when I was with him, he stopped by the Club. A short, well-built young Pathan man greeted him modestly. He was in his early twenties, but looked younger, barely postpubescent, and had just a wisp of hair on his upper lip. Aurangzeb made small talk for a few minutes, then arranged for a time to meet.

"That was Jamil," he explained as we drove away. "I haven't seen him for a few weeks, and he looks hot and ready."

Yet we also spoke also about Haider as he drove, and Aurangzeb's concern for his welfare. As we talked, it became clear that the only way to save Haider was to get him out of the country and far away from his oppressive family environment. Aurangzeb had already thought about this, and had sent for application forms from several American vocational colleges, which had low admission standards.

When I left Karachi, the forms had not yet arrived.

I found out later that Haider had been accepted into a college in Orlando, Florida, due in large part to Aurangzeb's help and influence. After he had arrived, I spoke with him on the telephone on several occasions at Aurangzeb's behest. I assured him that I was ready to provide him help and support as he adjusted to life in the U.S. We found that we could talk quite easily on the phone, and he opened up to me, describing his life and the problems he was encountering.

Haider found his carnal desires difficult to contain. He would spend numerous evenings at the local bars and pick up men for sex. His studies suffered. In one conversation he told me that he had discovered Manhattan and was now flying up to New York regularly on weekends. He would spend the night in the seamy side streets and bathhouses of Greenwich

Village. Haider was transformed; he had even taken up smoking and drinking. He told me he liked New York and was considering a move there. I would express my concerns to him when I spoke, but I was far too busy myself to invest the time it would have taken to reform him.

Eventually, he did move to the Big Apple, where took a job as bartender in the Village. He was young and attractive and life had become a big party for him. He loved sex and, as he explained boldly to me on the phone, he loved to get fucked. The true test of romance for him, he said, was a big, hard cock deep inside him, and strong arms tightly around him. He preferred his men to be physically large, to be well hung, and to use him at will for their sexual needs.

"I love the big, firm bodies of black guys here in New York," he exclaimed in one conversation. "And they can fuck hard. Just last night, I had a beefy hairy Italian who was so passionate. Do you think all Italians are like that? And then there are the Puerto Ricans—what dreamy eyes! And the blondes from Boston. God, so much variety. I guess I don't really care about type, as long as they are hard and can fuck forever." Then, he hesitated as if he suddenly realized he had been talking to Aurangzeb's friend. "I really miss Aurangzeb, still, and sometimes when I am being fucked, I think about him."

Over time I lost track of Haider. He moved and his forwarding phone number was disconnected. He did not call. Also, Aurangzeb had also stopped receiving any correspondence from Haider, and his letters to him went unanswered.

Years later I heard news of Haider quite by accident. A friend in Toronto, an expatriate New Yorker, had a visitor from his hometown who was a childhood friend. On meeting me and learning that I was from Karachi, Alan exclaimed, "Hey, I knew another gay Pakistani—a man named Haider." I was astonished.,

"He and I were boyfriends for awhile. Do you know anybody named Haider?"

I nodded. "Do you still keep in touch with him?"

There was that long hesitation full of uncomfortableness. "He died. AIDS."

Alan told me he had been at Haider's bedside in the final days.

Haider had been unable to consistently practice safe sex, Alan said, even after there was overwhelming evidence about the modes of HIV transmission. He required his sex partners to wear a condom when he was sober, but would lapse when drunk, which was often. Alan had scolded him about it, but Haider cheerfully waved his concerns away.

"Pakistanis are immune to such diseases," he said to Alan. "I lost an aunt to tuberculosis and only three of my five siblings survived. This disease is no big deal. I am not worried. I can handle it."

After he found out definitively that he was sick—the Kaposi sarcoma lesions were visible and impossible to ignore—Haider refused to inform his family.

"It is better that I die quietly," he said. "I don't know what to say, or how to tell them. What difference will it make, anyway? I'll die on my own. Just cremate me and flush the ashes down the toilet."

Ultimately, he died alone, with a few close friends by his side.

Haider had been a generous and loving soul. They held a memorial and scattered his ashes along the Hudson River.

In a Muslim country like Pakistan, birth and death are both communal events. Each marks an important transition for the family. Births, especially of sons, are happy events, marked by the distribution of sweets and much celebration.

Under Muslim law and Pakistani custom, a dead person is to be buried quickly. As death occurs, the first important task is to get word out—to friends and relatives, to business associates, to neighbors, and to the entire community. Within hours, hundreds converge on the household to mourn and grieve. Men congregate in an area separate from the women, and the local mosque participates in providing *maulavis* to read from the Quran. The mourners console the family, recount stories about the deceased, and sympathize, weep and emote freely. There is genuine communal sorrow. All who are touched by the death are expected to show up, if at all possible, on the same day or shortly thereafter. This is not a simple formal visit; visitors from far away who fly in or take the train will sleep in the house—simple and effective arrangements miraculously materialize. Family feuds are suspended; long dormant relationships are revived. The focus of the event is the loss of the dead person, and note is taken of the fragility of life and human existence. Restraint is shed. The family's grief is shared, and the event is unfettered by niceties. The meaning of life is questioned; those closest to the dead person absorb themselves in understanding their own lives and their performance. On the day of judgment, the archangel Gabriel[1] is supposed to recite each man's good and bad deeds aloud, as God renders judgment—heaven or hell. On the day of death, the final chapter has been written for the dear departed, and friends and family recount his or her virtues, perhaps to ensure that Gabriel does not forget the good deeds. Hoping, perhaps, that when their time comes, someone will take the time to similarly immortalize them in memory. To be present at this place at this time is to gain additional *sawab*—brownie points for

---

[1] Islam subsumes the prophets of Judaism and Christianity, and Muslims believe in their validity. This therefore includes Garbriel, or *Gibreel*.

admission to heaven. It is considered good and necessary to show up, participate, and be counted. The events after death are prescribed in the Quran: The dead person will now have his or her day in God's court; and the mourners will take stock of their lives and contemplate how they would fare, had they been the ones to go. Were they pious enough? Did they practice Islam, pray, and give alms to beggars? Were they kind and loving?

Everyone's day is just around the corner.

There is no food cooked at the house of the person who has died. Neighbors and friends deliver cooked food, take care of chores, and envelop the bereaved family in a cocoon of social love. Those who help are never forgotten, nor are those who stay away at this time: they are forever marked.

Within the day of death, the body is washed completely according to custom, and the *jinaza*, or burial procession, proceeds to the graveyard. The body, barely cold, is buried in a simple white cloth and lowered into a hole in the dusty earth. The mourning period extends for forty days, after which all are to go back to the job of living in this world, and to surrender the dead person's fate to God.

One of the worst fates to befall a dead man is to have no family by his bedside. To die alone is the ultimate horror. This is what happened to Haider, alone in Manhattan, in a tenement apartment with pneumonia, too sick to move, resisting the cold efficiency of a hospital, and cared for by his few friends, the ceaseless noise of Manhattan traffic close outside reminiscent of Karachi except for the language. In our meeting and phone discussions, it was clear that Haider was at heart very Pakistani. He loved his family, was a Muslim, and had experienced the rituals of life and death that made life a comfortable continuum. I wonder how he felt, knowing that he had surrendered his birth-identity for his need for love, and traded in the unconditional acceptance of family and community for vagabond romantic love and the transient pleasure of sex.

What terror must have engulfed him! What deep spiritual loneliness must have gripped him as he slipped hazily into the arms of God! Alan spoke of the conversations he had had with him, sitting by his bedside. Haider talked of his family and wept in love and memory of a past he had lost. He spoke of all the good memories he had of living in Karachi, the family dinners and *Eid* celebrations, the simple pleasures and problems. He spoke of trips to the beach at Clifton, the *mela*[1] at which he had fallen off a ride and broken his arm as a child, and a schoolteacher he had had a crush on. Like a child, he had relived his innocent youth, relived the days before a Faustian bargain brought him to a strange land with strange assumptions about life.

Though he had adapted to life in America, in the final chapter of his life, he yielded to memories of earlier chapters, and Alan had listened in fascination and anguish. Freed from his libido, Haider had become a shy and gentle person. As a Muslim, he said he did not fear death; rather, his concerns had been to minimize the strain he put on others around him, and to go quietly.

Despite his anguish at dying alone, his greater fear was the effect that his unpalatable mode of death would have on his family. He was concerned that it might affect his sister's ability to marry, his brother's business prospects, and his family's reputation. Alan, who had long abandoned his Missouri roots and rarely spoke with his parents, found it incomprehensible that

---

[1] Fair.

Haider could harbor such mundane concerns while facing imminent death.

"Let me call your parents," he had pleaded. "They should know!"

But Haider was adamant. He made him promise not to tell them how he had died, but to cremate him and then tell them that he had drowned accidentally while on a camping trip. They would not ask for details or a police report, Haider told Alan; they just needed someone to explain how this happened, and reassure them in their grief.

"Please," Haider beseeched. "If you have ever loved me, do as I say. No one must ever know. My life may be over, but my family must go on untainted."

Now, unable to contain himself, Alan was relieved to reveal to someone who had known Haider in Pakistan what had really happened.

I told Aurangzeb the news. He was deeply affected. Though the years had passed and he had married and was raising a family, he still had fond memories of Haider, one of the few men he had truly loved. Aurangzeb had settled down in Karachi. His stable of men was now stocked with steady and dependable partners—he no longer had the time or inclination to cruise on a regular basis for entertainment. He had taken an apartment close to Bohri Bazaar, which he had furnished modestly and had maintained by a part-time servant.

"This is for my boys," he explained. "It is close to one of our business offices, and I have told my wife it is convenient to take a nap there in the afternoons. She asks no questions and, in fact, has never been there."

Aurangzeb had three children and was busy with his profession and his family life. He admitted that sex with his wife was infrequent, but she was happy: they lived well, and there was family around.

"There is more to life than just a hard cock, you know," he advised. "It is nice to be settled down, and you really should settle down too. There are plenty of men here if I feel like it, and I am sure my wife knows. But it really does not matter. It is not important to her or to me. We have a good family life, and it is nice for the children to meet their cousins and uncles regularly. It is truly wonderful to have a family, and I encourage you to consider it. Why live so far away and have to fight for your survival every day? You must consider coming back home to live, if it is not already too late. . . . Zebunnisa and I are planning a three-month trip to Europe next summer, perhaps we will swing by and see you in Toronto. That would be wonderful!"

The story of two men: Aurangzeb, who stayed behind and reformed to meet social expectations, and Haider, who sought freedom from culture and family and pursued his individuality, only to lose it in the end. This morality tale has a obvious message for the gay Pakistani man: do what you want, as long as you can come home, back to family. Freedom and liberty have their consequences, if the price you pay is to reject family. It is possible, within the family framework, to carve out a measure of freedom, and this is the right thing to do—irrespective of where in the world you are.

If Haider had stayed in touch with his family and with Aurangzeb, there is a good possibility that they could have "rescued" him from his isolation and loneliness in his final days, and provided him with the family contact he so desperately needed. But he had decisively severed his ties and remained adrift, far away. Even at death's door, he realized that he could not go back to plead his case, that he would be greeted as a shameless outcast rather than a prodigal son. He had crossed the line and could not return.

There are many in Pakistan today who know that marriage is wrong for them, because they are attracted only to men. Most are not as mobile as Haider, nor as worldly-wise as Aurangzeb. Some may leave their families completely, as did Haider; but the vast majority accommodate to the culture. They may delay marriage on various pretexts. Some may be successful in delaying it long enough that they can declare themselves unmarriageable, too set in their ways. In a city like Karachi, there are thousands of stories, and as many reasons and ruses. Ultimately, it is his family's concern for his welfare that propels a man into marriage, since unmarried men, it is unquestioningly thought, must be unhappy men.

If a man wants to systematically elude this chase, he can often do so. The question then becomes: what is he to do? Single adult men do not really have a social place. Unless they can find happiness in isolation, they must resign themselves to a small and pitied niche in society.

For many homosexually oriented men, marriage is a far more practical solution to the loneliness and isolation of an unmarried life. A man can marry and then search for men in public places or find companionship with other homosexual men. A double life is better than no life at all. Indeed, a double life is not quite as strained as it sounds. As Aurangzeb's example shows, there is ample freedom within the social framework for a man to freely seek the company of other men, for intimacy. There is no framework for an exclusive relationship with another man, but friendships can be very close, and a wide variety of arrangements can be quietly accommodated.

As I was to discover, same-sex relationships can be just as hard to attain, and harder to sustain, in North America. The independence attained by leaving must be balanced against distance from family, loneliness, and isolation, and the constant work required to build a network of friendships that is durable. The cost-benefit tradeoff is not as clear to most Pakistanis as it was for me. I found some Pakistanis who, like Aurangzeb, were relatively happy in the balance they had struck in their lives. I found yet others who, lacking the means—psychic or material—to strike out on their own, envied what they fancied was my ability to do as I wished. They did not quite understand that this freedom was earned, and that liberty, as Haider's example shows, extracts its price.

A Fresh Start

The question of identity played a major part in my "decision" to settle outside Pakistan. It was not really a conscious decision, but a choice that revealed itself only over time. There was no specific time at which I assembled the facts, set the criteria, and considered the alternatives in any systematic way. Rather, as time went by, there was an osmotic process whereby I absorbed the fundamental individualistic values of North America and slowly shed the more egregious sentimental vestiges of home.

There are several questions to consider here. The word "settle" implies a stationary and stable center of gravity, and my lifestyle does not conform to any such reassuring locus. I have rarely spent more than a few months without traveling for at least a few days, for business or pleasure, and often abroad. For me, settling is a mental state, a conceptual, emotional and political center of gravity that one temporarily accepts as the center of one's universe. It helps to have a home with immovable heavy objects, like furniture, and financial constraints, such as mortgages. To fill the day, it helps to have comfortable schedule, friends in a social circle, a profession that holds promise, and daily challenges of the mundane kind, such as selecting a restaurant, rearranging the furniture, making love, searching for love, and similar distractions. In this state, one is considered "settled" unless something unsettling happens.

And so it was, with this set of criteria, I settled down in Toronto. As I mentioned, my identity had a great deal to do with this decision. From a purely financial viewpoint, I could have been more successful in Karachi. With well-connected friends like Aurangzeb, memberships in the right clubs, and occasional work, I could easily afford biannual jaunts abroad, to shop, consume, and simulate decadence before slipping back into respectable Karachi life. However, such a life would require a wife, family, and a socially constrained existence. That was baggage that I had been unwilling to carry.

My life in Toronto was hardly an integrated and holistic delight. I posed as a professional by day and socialized with gay friends by night and on weekends. I was a hardworking bachelor within the expatriate Pakistani community. I had little in common with many of these people, some of whom were economic refugees. Most Pakistanis I met were from backgrounds that were substantially different from mine, though the food they served was invariably good, and meeting them in familiar settings struck a sentimental chord. My straight professional friends, with few exceptions, knew nothing of my romantic interest in men. And the typical workweek left little time for love, just occasional sex. Although my search criteria were fuzzy, it was obvious that most prospective partners I met were unsuitable for a serious relationship. Over time, I learned to transform loneliness into independence. My romantic liaisons were generally superficial and temporary, so I learned to enjoy them, as intense, but fleeting, moments of passion. I had succumbed to pragmatic accommodation.

There is no unified culture in Toronto to compete with the culture I had grown up in. The Pakistani community here replicates Pakistani life where possible. Little nuclear families socialize with other little nuclear families, and coalesce to form little communities. These communities hold social events, conduct classes in Islamiat[1] for children, and argue over dinner about Pakistani politics. The unwritten rules of Pakistani life and morality are observed: women's first priority is their children; after fulfilling this, or if they cannot have children, they are able to work. Girls lead conservative lives, and no dating is permitted. Children are expected to focus on their studies. Material success is important, though the ostentatious display of such wealth is considered in poor taste among many Pakistani professionals.

Class differences are important, just as they are in Pakistan. Because it was a relatively small community, there was only a small subset that broadly fit my particular profile. These professionals are in turn self-conscious of their ties to family in Pakistan and of their ambitions here, and eager to chart a course that would assure them success beyond what they could have achieved had they not ventured abroad. We may have had a some background in common, but little in terms of goals. We would meet warily from time to time, talking, networking, and assessing each other's advances. The men would discuss male things, like family and jobs, the women would compare their husbands' successes and those of their children. This was exclusively a heterosexual world, an alien landscape where I was seeking a beachhead.

The fragmentation of my life deepened. I had a full menu to choose from, in any given week: gay or straight, Pakistani or

---

[1] Religious schooling.

Canadian, to commune or to advance professionally, to search for a partner or to socialize. It was exhausting. I had chosen the life of an expatriate in search for liberty from social dogma, and my escape to freedom had yet to yield any tangible benefits.

I could always go back home, I reasoned.

I fancied that this back door was always available to me; that I could always wrap up my affairs, jump on a plane and go back home. Yet, as time passed, it became increasingly clear that I was now deeply anchored, and that a simple return home was out of the question. I was an immigrant and would have to take the good with the bad.

Constructing my life as a gay man, with raw materials that were new to me in a community that was inherently foreign to me, provided a novel mix of challenges. Foremost among these was the inherent transience of all my states of equilibrium. In Pakistan, I had seen the stable life trajectories of men around me: the seven ages of man acted out from birth to old age and anchored in a firm foundation. In Canada, everything seemed provisional, an adventure. All relationships seemed fragile; all institutions, distant; and all beliefs, transient. Jews converted to Christianity, and Christians became Buddhists. Families were groupings of convenience, to be abandoned for personal goals. Everything was frantic, and everyone was conventional. Indeed, the much-advertised "freedom" of the individual actually limited individual freedom. People were labeled by the views they expressed, how they looked, what they wore. To avoid undesired labels, I saw friends act out in daily life the stereotypes they sought to emulate: the busy executive, the radical leftist, the frothy adolescent. Normative behavior was heavily marketed, in advertising, consumer goods, and social behavior. In Pakistan the social classes were relatively immobile: there was little an individual could do to spoil things. You could walk in public in mismatched pajamas, pick your nose, advocate communism, and even discreetly meet men for sex. None of this was construed as a fundamental blemish. In Canada, on the other hand, every expression of individual belief or behavior was seen in the context of group affiliation: you were gay, communist, or a social misfit. To avoid such labels, the upwardly mobile lived desperately bland lives, with politically correct affiliations, such as Greenpeace or Amnesty International. The radicals marched against the war or for gay rights, while others stood on the sidelines, knowing that their social dossiers were at stake. In South Asia, nothing changes quickly except through cataclysmic events. Therefore, the advocacy of change by an individual is an amusing exercise, not to be taken seriously. In North America, power is dynamically negotiated, and every seriously proposed alternative is considered for backing by others and potentially a legitimate challenge to the status quo. This fundamental attribute of a free society is difficult for a native Pakistani to fully engage.

On more than one occasion in Pakistan, when I was asked what I found most attractive about living in North America and I answered "freedom," the reply was: "But you are perfectly free to do anything you want here! Why would you want to leave and go abroad?" It was difficult for people in Pakistan to understand that I valued freedom for others and, as a consequence, valued my own freedom. I found that I had absorbed the egalitarian ideal, even as the Canadian middle classes around me indulged in rampant consumerism in an effort to appear successful and destined for the upper classes. Ralph Lauren extracted from frantic yuppies pressing the limit on their Visa cards a twofold premium for his T-shirts celebrating the leisure-class game of polo. Benetton plastered its logo on bright colors that clung to the tight, velvety chests of beautiful boys at the

Toronto bar, Buddies, while Swatch watches and designer sunglasses completed the tableau. This *faux* lifestyle had so little to do with the real thing, yet, it was in this milieu that I had to search for love, to justify my pilgrimage away from home.

Unlike some others of Muslim background, I have kept my given name. It is a Muslim name. It fits in naturally in Karachi, but sounds foreign in Canada and seems impossible for others to spell or pronounce. It appears to some to be a political act to retain it, but I have never considered changing it, or using a supplementary Christian name. My name marks me as a Muslim, and living in a society centered around group-identity politics, I have often served as a proxy representative for the billion Muslims of the world when there is an event, typically a crisis, in which Muslims play a role. I have felt that if I were to change my name to Dave or Joe or John, that it would change me dramatically. The last vestige of historical identity would snap, and I would be just another Charlie wandering down Main Street, sharpshooting for the jackpot. Perhaps this would be a good thing and would enable me to shed the yoke of the past and venture unencumbered to create my destiny, like the original settlers in this New World. Perhaps identity, history, and memories of culture are all baggage to be disposed of to lighten the boat of life and enable it to seek swifter streams. After all, what was there about my past that was noble and worth retaining?

I also found, however, as I looked further into the question of religion, that the principles of Islam are embedded deep within me. I am a Muslim and could not change that fact even if I had wanted to. Islam is a way of life, and it was my life through adolescence. Just as vivid family memories are etched within my mind, and just as early sexual awakenings create indelible marks, so growing up within a Muslim community made me love the religion at a very fundamental, unconscious level, as a part of who I was. I was not practicing its tenets—I intellectually rejected the notion of God. Muslim communities had, at best, an inferior role for those such as me who do not create families; and yet, I saw in myself a mirror image of the culture and environment that nurtured me during my formative years.

With the advantage now of a bird's-eye view, I can see how Islam as practiced in the most Muslim countries shutters out the modern world, in sharp contrast to the period in the past when Islam was, in fact, the modern world. The Islam that represented liberal ideals, rational scientific inquiry and intellectual conquest during Europe's Dark Ages is the same Islam that exists today, at least on paper. The Quran and Hadith are unchanged. Why, then, has Islam seemingly slipped into its own dark ages? Why are Muslims depicted as Arab boors, Iranian terrorists, and mindless Mullah-trodden nonentities? Many here in my adopted land (and in the superpower to its south) think that I have escaped the "chains of ignorance" of an Islamic lifestyle and am now basking in the "light of freedom" that created McDonald's, free speech, gay liberation, and the bomb.

Shed the past! Change your name, like those at Ellis Island in New York. After all, the Jews that changed their names in order to "pass" in anti-Semitic New York after the war did not become any less Jewish as a result. They adapted! Why not exhibit a similar resilience?

The Islam of my childhood had clear and kind values, and noble ideals that I perceived to be practiced by those around me. In fact, it was rife with what are supposed to be "Christian virtues."

Ahead of me lay the biggest challenge of all: the search for love. And such a search could start only if I were to identify who I was to myself. This search for identity was buried in my life in Toronto. It was too much like home. Toronto's gay ghetto was forbidden to me: it was too close to home, and I could not be seen there. Ultimately, it took a *hejira*[1] to California for me to experience for the first time the alternatives available to me, and to fall in love with a man for the first time. But before that, I had to play out a vital chapter in my life, necessary for all Muslims. I had to marry.

---

[1] Journey. *Hejira* also refers to the journey that Mohammad, the prophet of Islam, took from Mecca to Medina.

Fulfilling My Duty

My family expected me to get married. No surprise! On each trip home, I was introduced to potential brides. Aunts who had access to potential matches for me to inspect materialized mysteriously at tea time. This was eminently reasonable, of course. I was a good catch, of marriageable age, well educated and with a good job. Also important, I lived in Canada, which meant that I was liberated, or at least would consider granting a wife some measure of personal freedom.

I was also adept at refusing prospective candidates, for various reasons. This was not difficult, since every girl I met had potential flaws and every family had its shortcomings. Ultimately, the calendar always came to my rescue: I had to return to Toronto, and there was never enough time.

"Get married before you get too old," they would all urge. "You deserve to be happy. Don't be afraid! Once you find a nice girl, you will wonder why you waited all this time. Find a young girl! She will create healthy children for you. Do not worry so much. It is natural to get married! Don't wait too long, or you will be an old man with young children! Toronto. is so cold. She will keep you warm!"

This cat-and-mouse game continued over several visits. They would try to persuade me, for my own good. I would resist. Everyone would assume that this was simply a case of stage fright or of unrealistic standards. Perhaps the girl was not pretty enough, or the family not distinguished enough. Then it would be countdown to departure, and I would escape.

Gradually a barely perceptible change came over me. My defenses against getting married started to crumble. As I approached thirty years of age, I began to see the wisdom in what was being suggested. I decided I could work around the issue of sexual attraction and commit myself to a public life as a married family man. In private, I reasoned that I could occasionally satisfy myself with men. This was my opportunity to join the mainstream, and I should take it.

Life in Canada was not easy. My professional life was adequate, though not progressing as I thought it should. I had a few friends, but none who I could count on as I looked into the future. Ostensibly, I was settled and modestly successful. But there was a void in my life. I had no one to love, no one to share my feelings with, and no children to point the way to the future. How could I consider myself settled in a mature way when I was so alone?

When my bed was shared, it was generally with a man. It fact, this was usually the case. There were, however, a few exceptions. In all these cases the woman had found me attractive, seduced me, and we had sex. My hands had roamed her body, my penis jerked to erection, I had lowered my then-angular body over hers and entered an already moist cavity. A few motions, a little stroking, and it was over. Once, a multi-orgasmic woman had frightened me with her passion as she clawed my back with her ruby-red talons, moist vaginal fluid lubricating both our midsections. None of these women were adept at fellating me, and my interest in stroking and massaging their pudenda was limited. So it was generally a case of erection into orifice, friction, ejaculation, and a stiff drink afterwards. However, these experiences taught me that while I did not find women to be intrinsically attractive, I could function sexually with them. Their large loins were designed to absorb my sperm and create babies. Their soft bosoms were snugly pillows that would bloom and fill with milk to nurse my children. My babies would be mine; they would be connected biologically to me, and I would feast in their sight, smell, piss, shit and vomit. My son, my son . . . he would look like me, and I would be biologically fulfilled.

I wanted my son. I wanted him now, instantly. But to have him, I reasoned, I would need a cooperative woman who would breed with me, and cheerfully take care of all the hard work for me. In other words, I needed a Pakistani wife. If she would raise my family, then I would do whatever it took to take care of her as part of the bargain. She would never need to see me as anything but the loving, caring husband that I would transform into. In retrospect, this was naïveté, but it may well have worked with the right woman.

Also there was a profound ethical aspect to this. How could I get married, knowing that I was sexually attracted to men? How could I "use" another person in this way, just to create a family? As I think back to that time, I did not envision a choice in the matter, nor did I see the conflict between getting married and my attraction to men. I was programmed to act the way I did and, while it may now appear to be a pitiful excuse, at that time it was neither a reason nor a justification. There was no thought at all given to the alternative of not getting married.

Perhaps the ethical issue relates to Pakistani society programming its men to believe that there is no option to marriage. However, most relationships have a calculated foundation, so if I did get married to raise a family, was that wrong? Would it have been less wrong if I had married my wife for her money instead? Since I consider myself fundamentally ethical, this question concerns me, now that I am less innocent and more thoughtful.

I resigned myself to an arranged marriage. Systematically, I studied the necessary parameters: age, education, family background. I gave thumbs up to the Karachi team: *Okay, I was ready to get married. Find me a suitable woman. Let's get on with it.*

Choosing A Wife

Once I had made the decision, the rest was remarkably easy. I would liken it to choosing a pair of suitable shoes while one is barefoot. Compromises are readily made, and in the fantasy world of an arranged marriage, too much knowledge is unnecessary and a dangerous thing. Everything is ultimately expected to work out, and what cannot be made to work is tolerated.

I met several girls. These meetings were always intermediated by family, friends, or relatives who had introduced their own marriageable daughters, or had an interest in tracking my progress. The initial meetings almost always had a somewhat surreal quality about them. There would be tea and snacks. I would sit with the men, and discuss the weather, while presenting my credentials. Impressed, they would present their family's background and discuss their own occupations. Often the first meeting would be the last, since my family or I surfaced a legitimate problem with the family, their attitudes, their background, or status. Or the other family decided to withdraw, for unspecified reasons that were probably just as irrational. This would happen even before the candidate-bride showed her face. If matters progressed smoothly and the girl joined the gathering, she would be grilled by my female family members and summarily rejected as not good enough. Finally, the field narrowed, and a girl was chosen who came from a "good" background and was suitably pretty. I regarded the choice favorably.

Nusrat was just nineteen and in medical school in the M.B., B.S. program at Dow Medical College in Karachi. She wanted to go abroad, and was uncertain of her desire to continue medical education. My sister pointed out that Toronto had some of the finest universities in Canada and that she could enroll in a suitable pre-med program. While Nusrat was twelve years younger than me, she appeared mature and ready, and her family seemed interested in arranging a suitable match. She was attractive, well groomed, and her family members were successful professionals. She was introduced by a matchmaker and, while our families had no prior connection, she was within the acceptable social range.

Our first meeting was at Nusrat's family's house in a remote section of the city Nazimabad, with perhaps a dozen people present. It was a large room, with mismatched furniture that had obviously been uncovered for the event. The curtains were musty and threadbare. The smell and formal layout of the room suggested that it was little used, which marked this meeting as a special occasion. Ornate lamps stood mismatched on *faux* marble-topped tables, and freshly dressed servants darted about, serving tea and snacks. Everything had to be just right. The *grande dame* of the house was accompanied for the occasion by her complete family *sans* husband and one daughter.

"He is at work, and she is at college," she explained. This was clearly a family occasion, a social meeting, with deeply personal undertones. It was a serious affair, masquerading as a tea party.

The men were ushered to one section of the room, the women to another. I sat in an armchair, in a position of honor. I had already been screened through the grapevine and found to be adequate. Now the question was one of chemistry. Not just the chemistry between me and the woman who would potentially share my bed, but the chemistry between the families. What was on the table was a lifelong relationship. These men would call me "brother" and be forever in my sphere. These women would show their faces forevermore at important events that called for social contact and would visit me at will. This was a diplomatic meeting, a high-level conference. Briefing books had been studied, advisors consulted, and scenarios for success and failure discussed. We knew their family background for two generations, as they did ours. Friends and acquaintances, however distant, were referenced to helpfully fix coordinates and establish credentials.

This was women's work. I could hear the discussion from a distance. They asked questions that were direct and often personal. This was no time for delicacy, since a serious step was about to be taken. This was a heavily choreographed investigation: every word, every pause, every delicate hesitation conveyed opinion, position, and circumstance. It came naturally to these women. After all, social life is the mainstay of life in Pakistan, and such skillful negotiation and navigation is an essential part of this life. Within the hour, the women had sized up whether they had friends in common, and what opinions they held of people known through reference. This vetting process help create esteem and affection between our two families regardless of whether I married Nusrat. This was constructive activity, busy bees tending to the social hive, building each tier with delicacy and tact. One unwarranted word could sour the situation at this stage.

The men, meanwhile, were casually discussing manly things. I was asked about life in Canada, my work, and the political situation in Pakistan. We spoke of the weather and the demands of travel. One of her brothers had a friend in Vancouver: Did I know him? Another mentioned a relative at New York University: Had I run into him? Did I participate in the Pakistani social organizations in Toronto? Did I cook for myself or eat out? Work was hard, they knew, but everyone has to make time for leisure. How did I spend my free time? All casual questions that new acquaintances may ask. But I knew without a doubt that after we left, if there was continued mutual interest, phone calls would be made, references in Canada and the U.S. checked, and any blemish in my background would be cause for rejection. If the matter was to proceed further, an informal task force would be assembled from within the family network in deadly earnest. The men at the helm would probe, investigate, verify, validate, and flush out the slightest hint of scandal or impropriety in my background. Undoubtedly there were friends or family, or family members with friends or family, in the Toronto area. They would investigate me, verify employment, street address, and lifestyle. This benign social occasion was the start; they wanted to see if I was truthful. In turn, I asked the questions that were expected. I inquired about their educational backgrounds, business standing, travel abroad, views about politics, society, and values. Were these the kind of men I would want to spend my life around? Were they open-minded and sincere, possessed of character and stature? Through such inquiry, my job was to deduce whether I would be compatible with their sister. A teacup and a small plate laden with sweets and samosas in hand, I played my part in this drama.

While we were talking, I heard Nusrat's mother excuse herself. She returned in a few moments, daughter in hand. Nusrat was introduced to my sisters and mother. This was a good sign. It showed that we had passed the first cut. This was clearly a modern and enlightened family, since it was rare for the girl to display herself before a suitor. I heard my mother and sister greet her, and I turned to look. She sat down without a glance in my direction, her side to me, so that I could see her profile and see the movement of her head and body as she spoke. This was my moment to assess whether she was adequately attractive. The talk had turned casual, the business agenda for this meeting was over. After another half hour of discussion during which my sisters chatted with Nusrat, we departed.

"So, what did you think of her?" my sister asked.

"Looks quite good," I said, clearing the way for further overtures.

I would meet Nusrat again, twice more, and speak directly with her just once. At our second meeting, her brother informed me that "a good friend" of his was in Toronto and I must look him up when I returned. He had clearly been busy between our meetings. My conversation with Nusrat at our third meeting was brief. She had a pleasant smile, and deep dark eyes. She was slender, short, and fair-skinned, a girl. Her voice was somewhat high pitched. She was tense, but had an expressive face. I asked her how she liked the weather, and told her that I was visiting from Toronto. After a few moments, her mother came over and protectively led her away, like a dainty flower in risk of withering from too much exposure. We never met in private before we were married.

I returned to Toronto, having given permission for a marriage proposal to be made on my behalf. It was accepted. We had both passed the hurdles, and the course was set for the finish line. I was engaged, and the marriage was scheduled for the following month. I would fly to Karachi, get married the day after, pick her up, and fly back with her a week later. The visa paperwork had been arranged, to make this possible. I was excited, relieved, and happy in a primal sense, I had surrendered to what I instinctively knew was right. At no point was I concerned that it was dishonest not to disclose to her my attraction to men. That was a separate issue entirely and would not prevent me from being a good husband. I was convinced of that.

Bride and Bridegroom

I landed at Karachi airport and was greeted effusively by my old family, as well as my new one. Her brothers greeted me with respect, and large garlands and necklaces of rose petals were draped around my neck. I had been invited to join their family. There was much affection exchanged and relief that the girl was about to be married off to someone who appeared to be such an excellent choice.

Exhausted by the trip and time-zone changes, I slept into the next day. The wedding was to be held at the Beach Luxury Hotel, close to the bay. Several hundred guests had been invited. There would be a banquet that evening, at the home of a family friend, who lived in the Defense Society. This was all to be arranged and paid for by Nusrat's family.

Later, she and I would check into the hotel for our first night together. Two days later, a *valima* reception would be hosted by my family. This would mark consummation of the marriage and our acceptance of Nusrat as part of our family.

Her *jahaiz*[1] would be moved to our house and, henceforth, she would live with me.

The marriage was a large and public affair. The rich and oily food was plentiful. Flashbulbs snapped continually, assuring that the occasion would be fully documented. Married friends came up and hugged me with deep affection; I was about to join the circle. Unmarried male friends nudged me to confirm that I had slept well and was "ready"—thinly veiled allusions to the promise of the sexual exhaustion to come and the promise of unfettered sexual satisfaction, which they lacked and was now mine. Female relatives giggled and told me she was really attractive and predicted that I would be happy. Friends of my father hugged me and wished me luck. It was a festive and upbeat affair.

I was dressed in a new *sherwani* suit and sat on a makeshift stage on a sofa. She was dressed in a brocade gown, her face veiled as she sat beside me. The wedding itself was quite simple, as we had agreed in advance. The *maulavi* reviewed the previously agreed *nikah*[2] contract. We both signed. The witnesses, two males, also signed. Officially, we were then married. The crowd milled about, and then there was a mad rush for the food.

Cherry Picking

The hotel room was overdecorated and gaudy. The wedding bed was covered with rose petals. She was now alone with me. This stranger—dressed in multilayers from head to toe, smelling of sweat and perfume—was now my wife.

---

[1] Dowry.
[2] Marriage.

She sat on the chair, head cast downwards. This must have been the most fearful moment of her life. I sat on the bed nearby. We sat in silence for a few minutes. I took her hand in mine, stroked it. Each finger was ringed, and her palm was covered in intricate *mehndhi*[1] patterns. I slowly removed her veil, then raised her chin gently with my hand. She glanced at my eyes, turned a bright red, and again cast her gaze downward. This was our first night as man and wife, and the task before us was to consummate the marriage. We were both tired, but well aware of the requirements. I had to make her mine, to possess her.

I helped to undress her. She seemed so fragile, so tentative, and so shy. After the gold, brocade, lace, and shoes had been removed, she covered herself with her hands and, underclothes still on, darted into bed. I removed my clothes, and got in on the other side of the king-sized bed.

With the lights off, I let my lips wander over her cheeks. I removed her bra, with her help. With my prompting, she removed the rest of her underclothes.

I was hard. Leaning over, I jabbed in approximately the right place. She cried, then moved a bit. I jabbed again, feeling the soft hair of her mound brush against my swollen head. She caught my shoulders, her long painted nails bit deep in. It hurt. With one quick push, I tore open her door, and she screamed in verification. I was in. Halfway home, I slowly slid into the warmth, as she lay gasping and moaning. Her legs opened completely, as she surrendered to her husband's prerogative.

Afterwards, she slipped out silently to wash. She returned wearing a nightgown and entered the bed. Since we slept on different sides of the bed, I didn't notice the dampness. But in

---

[1] Henna.

the morning, the sheet was a bright red, evidence of her carnal purity. Her underclothes, curled in a ball in the bathroom, were also blood red. I kissed her forehead, she called her mother, and she asked my permission to go back to see her family that evening. I refused, in my first act of asserting my dominance as a husband. She pleaded, and I consented after a while, but set conditions: she could leave to return to her family's house only after we had had lunch at my house, and subject to my mother's permission. She was now my wife, and it was my job to set suitable limits.

The conditions were *pro forma* and my mother readily agreed to them. Her family arrived to pick her up for the evening, returning her later to sleep with me. We were both exhausted. There were events yet to happen, such as the *valima*—the wedding reception. Most important, though, there was work to do. I had just three days to prepare for our departure, to say all our good-byes, and to complete the immigration formalities for Canada. My wife and I, woman and man, had married and had consummated our marriage. Her bloodied bed sheet was taken to be washed, and we had presented the evidence of her virginity and my sexual potency to the world. The process was done. We were now a family unit. I was deeply satisfied.

How could I have wished for anything else?

Married Life

We had applied for her immigration to Canada the day after our wedding. We discovered then that she would have to wait in Karachi for the papers to clear, after which she could join me in Toronto. I was able to help expedite the process somewhat, but it was impossible for us to fly back together.

When I returned to Toronto, I informed my friends that I was married and was warmly congratulated. And I cleaned my house, spending hours reading and tearing up old letters, and throwing away pictures of men from my past. I was beyond the frivolous early stages of my life. I was now an adult, a married man. I looked forward to joining the conventional mainstream and raising a family.

She arrived just six weeks later. We rapidly settled in to a busy life. Nusrat was young and adaptable and quickly learned the methods of Toronto. The non-working wives in the local Pakistani community helped her find the right shops, taking her around while I was at work. Her cultural adaptation was swift. Rather than immediately enter college, she wanted to wait for perhaps a year, to acclimate more completely.

Needless to say, my life had changed completely. I no longer saw my old friends. Instead, much of my free time was spent coordinating home matters or entertaining her friends, wives of Pakistani men in the community, women who could help her to settle in quicker.

I learned very quickly that Nusrat was quite the opposite of the shy and demure girl I had met on my wedding night. When I came home exhausted from work, she would want to go out to dinner and then go dancing. Instead of sympathy and consideration, there were ceaseless demands and complaints. I did not earn enough money to satisfy her needs. She loved to shop and was constantly discussing what she had seen that she wished she could buy, were I more financially successful. After visiting friends for dinner, she would discuss their tastes and furnishings derisively. After we had visitors, she would complain bitterly about how we lived in a dump. She decided that she did not wish to pursue her college and medical studies after all. That could wait. She was young and wanted to enjoy life in the present. I could not persuade her otherwise.

She demanded sex constantly. She would be dressed up and perfumed, ready for me when I returned home from work. If I was anything short of enthusiastic, she would complain that I did not want her anymore. She would mention characters in the soap operas she had watched during the day, to establish her frame of reference. "You should see Brad and Annie on *The Guiding Light*. He's so sweet to her."

She hated Toronto, she said, and wished she could return home. But if she had to be here, she wished we could lead a better life.

When we had company for dinner, or were visiting with friends, the picture she presented was in stark contrast to the views she expressed privately. She would proclaim her happiness, her satisfaction with life in Toronto, her contentment with me as a husband. Everything was fine, and she was adapting well to her new environment. It must have appeared to all in the community that we were a perfect couple.

Her family, however, knew better. She would spend hours on the telephone to Karachi, mostly complaining about how she missed her friends, and how "cheap" I was. She complained that I would limit her spontaneity by suggesting that she shop for the best price, or that she wait for a sale. She said she felt trapped, because I had not bought her a car yet. Though she would call her family when I was not there, I overheard her more than once after returning home while she was on the phone. After these complaint sessions, she would be sweet and considerate. Perhaps her mother admonished her to be more patient and kind. On the occasions when I would talk with her mother on the phone, she would apologetically say that Nusrat was a bit high strung, that I should try to be patient.

"When she has children, she will settle down," she would assure me.

Sex with a woman is fundamentally different from sex with a man. Female sexual energy builds up more slowly, but once Nusrat was aroused, it was difficult to contain her passion. Her orgasms were tumultuous and frequent, and I was often spent while she was still charged up, sputtering like a sexual firecracker. Not only is the vagina a naturally moist and elastic cavity, but the soft fleshy body around the cavity moaned differently, moved differently, and came to orgasm differently. However, I adapted. Before long, I had arranged to reach orgasm in advance, and then stimulate her to reach multiple orgasms while I thought of dinner. It was wearisome, but a passing phase, I felt. We would bore of sex over time and focus on other things. I was perfectly content for sex between us to be a periodic cordial affair, after which we would perhaps have tea. Instead, she continued to be demanding, lusty, and exhausting. We finally settled into a weekly routine, adequate for me and boring for her.

Over time her behavior out of bed did not improve. She was moody and erratic when alone with me, and the perfect wife when in company. She threw temper tantrums. "God, I miss my family," she whined. "I wish I had never left home!"

Nusrat would become withdrawn, then bitter and spiteful. This became our routine. She specialized in Chinese take-out and watched endless soap operas for cultural training. Our relationship settled at a low plateau. She had befriended some sympathetic Pakistani women but, aside from seeing them, resisted my attempts to introduce her to my non-Pakistani friends and to take her to business-related social events where she could broaden her circle of acquaintances. Time passed slowly.

Two years after her arrival, Nusrat decided it was time for her to visit her family in Karachi for the summer. I consented. Once there, she extended her stay and, before long, fall was starting to chill into an early winter.

"Toronto is too cold to come back to, just yet" she opined. "I think I will stay here a bit longer. My father is not very well, and I must take care of him."

Thankfully, I agreed. It was surprisingly pleasant to have her gone. Her visit stretched out for six months, then into the following spring. Her father was improving, and she was taking care of him, she said. She informed me that she was not really in a rush to return to Toronto. Her mother tearfully told me that she had told her daughter that it was unwise for newlyweds to stay apart for so long, that I must be lonely without her, and that she would return shortly.

We would speak weekly and as the first-year anniversary of our separation approached, our conversations became more perfunctory. Our relationship was dissolving, held together neither by children nor by family, and made impersonal by distance. A few weeks later, I called Nusrat to tell her that I wanted a divorce, unless she returned immediately. There was much screaming in the background, with her father and brothers threatening her with unspecified consequences if she did not leave instantly to go back to her husband. I was calm and told her that she should do as she wished; I think some part of her expected me to beg her to come back. She grew hysterical when it became clear to her that she was dispensable.

"You don't love me!" she screamed. "You do not want to have any babies with me."

I hung up the phone and went to bed. I was strangely relieved that the matter had finally come to a head.

When she had been here in Toronto, Nusrat and I had talked frankly about when to start having children. Except for the wedding night and for a few days thereafter, I had used a condom as birth control. I had explained to her that I thought it would be wise to wait for some time, so that she could settle down, and also so that she could start studying again, to improve her English-language skills and attend college. She was still barely twenty, and I believed she would need some time to become comfortable with the new cultural and living environment before being burdened by children. She was quite pleased with this. I think she expected me to be less considerate of her needs and to want to start a family quickly. She had in turn discussed our plans with her mother, who had also assented to the wisdom of this approach. Nusrat then had herself fitted with a diaphragm, and I no longer used a condom. We both preferred the switch.

I had wanted her to adapt, so that she would feel confident within the mainstream culture. Despite my arranged marriage with a native Pakistani girl who had never before traveled abroad, I wanted for us to be able to avoid the inwardly focused ghettolike Pakistani immigrant community in Toronto. Our children would be Canadian first and Pakistani second. To ensure this, I tried from the start to interest Nusrat in joining me at performing arts events and other social gatherings that were largely Anglo-Canadian, and I encouraged her to invite non-Pakistani friends to our house. In the time that we lived together in Toronto, she resisted all these attempts. Instead, she encouraged me to go out alone. Initially I stayed at home to be with her, and limited our social life to the Pakistani community. As the second year progressed and the Christmas season was upon us, I finally decided that I had had enough. I accepted invitations to parties and social dinners on my own, and this extended the distance between us. Some of these invitations were to events hosted by gay friends. I was straddling not just the Pakistani and Canadian communities, but was also torn between the straight and gay worlds. I felt at home in gay circles, with friends I had known over the years, but I limited my interaction to social discourse and did not succumb to sexual temptation. To my credit, I consistently returned home to my wife.

As we drifted apart, she declared herself now ready to start a family. I disagreed and incurred her wrath by suggesting further delay. My sixth sense was telling me that a baby in our midst would forever bind us, and that she was not the person I wanted to be bound to. Even as we struggled with our relationship, the temptation to create a child was strong, though I despaired to come to terms with one of my fundamental reasons for getting married in the first place. This was a point of disagreement in our arguments, but I held fast. After it was clear that we were on opposite sides of this argument, I started to use a condom again, having lost trust in her claims to be continuing the use of her diaphragm. This further infuriated her. In retrospect, I believe I did the right thing, but occasionally I nostalgically think how nice it would be to have a child, born perhaps of a loveless marriage, but nonetheless my child, my flesh and blood, running around somewhere. A boy, of course.

I filed divorce papers. During this time, I was consoled by Pakistani friends, who professed not to understand what had gone wrong. Some of the women declared that Nusrat had never really settled down. They were right, of course, and their biased sympathies were with me. My parents, meanwhile, suffered through the anguish of my stillborn family unit, and then consoled me not to be disheartened by this failure. I told them that I would need to wait for some time before getting married again, to make sure I did not repeat the same mistake twice. They understood, although my father urged me not to wait too long, since I was already in my thirties.

This was a period of introspection and postmortem. What had gone wrong? Had I done the wrong thing by getting married in the first place? Had she figured out that I was not devotedly heterosexual, and had that somehow doomed the relationship? Had I done the right ethical thing by not disclosing to her that I had had sex with men, not just women, before we married? Should I have resisted her departure? Should we have had a child early, so that we would be cemented by more than personal compatibility? Should I get married again?

I finally resolved these questions in my mind to my satisfaction, for the moment. I had gone into the relationship with honorable intent and with goals reasonable for a Pakistani marriage. I had provided for her, and we had had an adequate sexual life together. She and I were not compatible, and there was no family to mediate. If I had made more skillful use of the extended Pakistani community in Toronto, perhaps that would have helped. But this aid could have come at the cost of burying us both in conservative convention. Ultimately, the relationship had fallen apart because we were simply two very different people, with different background, personalities, and expectations. In Pakistan, such a relationship would have limped along, supported by the extended family on both sides, and by the culture. In the isolated environment of Toronto, personal compatibility was a necessity. While sexual desire may not have been a prime factor, it certainly reduced my willingness to "stick it out." Arranged marriages work when those who arranged them are close by to smooth out the bumps. Otherwise, with two isolated individuals confined to an apartment, there has to be a deeper spiritual and emotional connection to foster intimacy and respect, irrespective of the carnal dimension.

I am glad, in retrospect, that we did not have children. I also resolved not to get married again. But if I were to consider it, I would definitely not attempt an arranged marriage.

I packed and shipped Nusrat's personal belongings back to her. My regret at her departure was balanced with great relief and a sense of freedom. My years with her had been a tumultuous period. Almost three years of my life had been invested in this venture to raise a family. However, the end of my marriage meant that I could decisively close this chapter of my life. I needed to start anew, with my true feelings as guide. I left Canada and went to California, the crucible of experimentation, to take the next clear step.

California, Here I Come

In 1980 I had an opportunity to spend a few months in San Francisco, then the known center of the gay universe. This was extraordinary good luck. I would have an apartment in the center of the Castro district which, as I discovered in an earlier preview trip, was a short walk from all the important gay bars I had read about. Seventeenth Street was just down the hill from Castro Street, and the stunning views and crisp air immediately drew me to the city.

The apartment building had a laundry room in the basement, shared by the tenants of its twelve units. On my first evening there, boxes unpacked, I trundled down to wash a load of laundry. Bag of dirty clothes in hand, I rounded a corner and almost bumped into a black man with beautiful eyes who was leaving.

"Excuse me! Sorry!" I hastily apologized.

"No problem." I saw his wide grin and his beautiful eyes started to flash. "You must be new in the building. Hi, my name is Greg."

He held out his hand, which I clasped. His palm was warm and soft, and his long slim fingers curled around the edge of my hand. Our hands fit well, and he gave me a long look before withdrawing his hand. We were standing in the doorway, frozen in time.

"So, where are you coming from?"

I told him Toronto.

"Wow, great! That is so far away. Well, welcome again! Which room are you in?"

I told him I was in room 7.

"That's right next door to mine! I'm in room 6. I have a great view. Listen, what are you doing later this evening? Why don't you stop by to say 'hi'?"

Intrigued, I said that I would.

He had a slim, taut body, and the most flagrant pair of bulbous buttocks I had ever seen. They jutted imperiously from the small of his back. His narrow waist and tight belly accentuated his broad shoulders. His shirt was partially unbuttoned, and I could see the smooth rich chocolate expanse of skin, undulating gently to the peaks of his nipples. He was small, shorter than me, but perfectly proportioned, except for his extravagant ass. He walked off, my admiring gaze following.

After completing my laundry, I felt the need to explore my new territory. I donned some running shorts and a T-shirt, and resolved to find out the hard way which muscles needed to be strengthened in order to become a jogger in San Francisco. I was tired, but Greg had invited me and I had promised to stop by. "I will apologize, and we will reschedule," I thought, knocking on his door.

"Who is it?" I told him it was me.

"Hi!" He opened his door, dressed now in pale blue shorts and a white T-shirt. "Come on in!"

"Actually, I stopped by to see if I could see you later, perhaps. I am a bit tired, and am planning to go for a run to unwind, and then I think I will just hit the sack."

"You look like you're ready for some serious exercise. I've got just the thing for you. Come in, come in! It is a great drink for instant energy."

I entered his apartment, which was tastefully decorated with rattan and bamboo, flowers and feathers. I would later discover that he frequented Cost Plus, a major importer of inexpensive home furnishings. The lights were dimmed, music played softly in the background. His musky cologne scented the air. He pursed his full, moist lips, as though pausing to think. I could see the undulations of his chest and belly through his T-shirt, and the visible pair of peaks just above where his firm nipples rode on his pulsating pectoral muscles. His shorts were loose, but I could not miss the jut of his ass, aligning perfectly with the graceful movements of his thighs and legs as he moved. When he turned toward me, I could see the shaft of his penis outlined beneath the cloth, and its location and movements were unmistakable. I could feel myself becoming tumescent.

He looked at me, and his eyes traveled down my body. His gaze lingered briefly at my crotch. Then, talking pleasantly, he turned to his kitchen area, opened his refrigerator, and poured me a drink.

"Here, try this."

I walked over to the kitchen area and took the drink from his hands. It seemed that almost before I raised the glass to my mouth, I felt my shorts being tugged down and, in one fell swoop, my cock was down his throat. I choked down a swallow of the drink, put the glass on the counter, and held his head against my crotch in sheer ecstasy. Without removing his mouth, he pressed his hand on my thighs and maneuvered me a few feet to his couch in the adjacent the living room. I leaned back on the couch, legs wide apart, while he was on his knees on the carpeted floor, his head moving over my crotch. It was after several minutes of expertly administered torture that I finally exploded in satisfaction deep in his throat. His mouth cradled my now-hypersensitive organ, skillfully avoiding friction, applying just enough pressure to squeeze laggard drops of semen through the system. He moved his body to the couch beside me, and I twisted sideways to permit him to lie on his back while my cock was still in his mouth. He was playing with his penis now, a huge, beautifully proportioned, black instrument, twice the size of mine. His shorts lay on the floor, long since discarded.

I watched him stroke himself, while my droopy organ lay captive in his moist oral cavity. I watched the contractions of his belly with each stroke of his hand, the upward lurch of his magnificent beast and its mighty round head. Instinctively, my hands reached for his balls, and he opened his legs wider, and raised them to help ease my journey. I reached for his ass and cupped it in my hand. It felt perfect, two halves of a peach, now open between his outstretched legs. I could feel the warm fire emanating from the crack between. Tentatively, I lowered a finger into this chasm and touched the rosebud, stroking it gently.

With a loud yell, he exploded in several jets. Semen blobs clung to his chest and filled the urn of his belly button. His body seemed engulfed in seizures, that lasted several seconds as cum continued to spurt. Finally the climax subsided, and he released my penis from his mouth.

I tugged up my shorts.

"Welcome to San Francisco," Greg said with a shy smile as he watched me prepare to leave. "Have a good run. See you soon."

I certainly intended to.

Greg's Cadillac

Greg epitomized the pleasures of casual sex. He had a beautiful body and he knew it, and a healthy appetite for sex, and he indulged it. His smooth, silky skin felt fine against my rough, hairy body, and he loved that. And, on our second encounter, he let me ride his Cadillac.

"Cadillac" was the name he had given his ass. This was no ordinary derriere, no run-of-the-mill posterior. True, it served the routine function of elimination. But it was the Mona Lisa of anuses, capped by the Mount Everest of buttocks. I marveled at its fine lines, its smooth, hard curves, and the ease with which it parted to reveal his entrance. Once inside, this work of art transformed itself into a mighty machine, soothing, pumping, squeezing, stroking, and nurturing the juices from its prey. Its grip was so tight that its permission was almost necessary to complete the simplest thrust. Yet its smooth and liquid walls applied salve to keep turgid the weariest of organs. On one occasion, it held me captive after I came and several minutes later coaxed me to an encore. All the while, his own organ was in full bloom, hanging long and heavy as it spurted in unison. Greg taught me that choreographed sex had its own special pleasures, that method could be rallied as an ally to lust, and that a systematic approach could, indeed, be rewarding. Each time we had sex, he exhausted me to satisfaction, and satisfied me to exhaustion. My organ limped back to my apartment after each bout, dragging my body along with it.

Greg typified one aspect of San Francisco—the sexual artist, the purveyor of fine sex. However, he knew of little else. He worked as a programmer at IBM, yet knew virtually nothing of the company's products. He enjoyed music and television, but could not name the governor of California. And Pakistan? He felt sure it was somewhere in the Middle East. He thought my name was cool, an affectation to avoid being an ordinary Joe. Relationships? He had had several very serious ones in just the past month, he told me.

This was true liberation! Sex was an art form, and Greg taught me that it could be practiced to high perfection. Greg blended attitude and showmanship to create the illusion of elegance and personality with a dramatic flair. However, it was clear after a few episodes with him that he lacked character, and had little notion of the concept. The services he rendered were limited. There was no more to him. Sex was more than just an act, and the intimacy it fostered created a bond between us that endured after I left his apartment. However, there was no residue of feeling that could be used to construct a foundation to any kind of enduring relationship. Sex was a satisfying workout for Greg and, while it was satisfying for me as well, it was not enough. I soon tired of him, and we eventually became casual friends and good neighbors.

And yet, I felt that this liberated city must also somehow enable sober gay men of character to create new ways of living. As I explored the city, I found that San Francisco had a gay community that included a wide variety of people, from a broad range of backgrounds. The ethnic list included Chinese and other East Asians, Mexicans and other Latin Americans, professionals who wore suits by day and disco danced by night, and businesses that catered to gay sensibilities. Unlike Toronto, where my life had been constrained by the Pakistani community and my gay friends invariably lived further away and operated in totally distinct social circles, in San Francisco there seemed to be a lot of overlap between the different communities.

I discovered gay catalogs, which listed gay doctors, gay accountants, and gay bankers. There were gay dry cleaners, gay bookstores, and gay theater. And this was not entirely a ghetto: At Halloween, non-gay friends and family members came out to join the gay community in celebration. It was, in fact, a community, as identifiable as any other and as open to newcomers as any other.

However, the focus of this gay "liberation" was white men, the mainstream majority. Non-whites were welcome, and Greg was an example. However, like many other American minorities, he was also dealing with issues of racism and discrimination, as he would explain to me the few times that we spoke about serious matters. This discrimination was not limited to the "straight" community, and Greg, whose sex partners were generally white, complained that even among the gay community this racism was always just beneath the surface, and sometimes above it.

The burden of carving an ethos for what it meant to be gay, and fighting for gay rights, was a white man's burden. Books, magazines, and erotic material all displayed and discussed issues from the white American man's perspective. The gay rights organizations that championed legal reform and backed candidates for political office were primarily white and overwhelmingly male. There were battles to fight with bigots in government, among religious leaders and right-wing thinkers who were all determined to classify same-sex love as unnatural and its practitioners moral degenerates. The spearheading of the gay-rights movement by white men was easy to understand, since power and wealth in American society were concentrated in the European-American majority. Just as the first demonstrations against the Vietnam war were by white Americans (even though a disproportionately high number of Afro-Americans were actually on the battlefield), so the battle against the injustice of discrimination against gays was first organized by the mainstream ethnic stake-holders, white Americans. The gay world in San Francisco mirrored the straight world in this important respect.

Other races were ornamentally displayed on the periphery. There was a group labeled Black and White Men Together,[1] for mixed-race couples. There were a few exotic clubs where non-whites tended to congregate: Oil Can Harry's attracted East Asians, and Esta Noche was Latino. The I-Beam attracted everyone to its throbbing beat. These venues were focused on fun. The outrage and moral fire that kept the leaders of the movement working with the exhausting zeal and energy that it took to win each battle was largely absent in these social clubs. Of course most white gay Americans also took a back seat and focused on sexual expression instead of political battle. But the fighting spirit and courage of the pioneering leaders of the gay movement were critical elements of the war against discrimination, and San Francisco was at the center of the battle.

I met no gay Pakistanis in San Francisco, nor did I find Muslims within the gay community then. In fact, by coming this far west, I seemed to have arrived in a place where background, religion, and culture seemed singularly unimportant. The core drive appeared at first blush to be hedonism, and I found the instant gratification of casual sex to be appealing and difficult to avoid. There was a little of Greg in everyone I met. Yet my

---

[1] It has since changed its name to Men of All Colors Together.

search for love was always just below the surface. And in this search, the introverted, Pakistani Muslim boy within me would never be far away, despite layers of experience and years of acculturation within the North American milieu.

Juan's Siren Song

Shortly after I left New York for Toronto, Pablo had left New York to settle in San Francisco. His PH.D. thesis was "still in process," as he would tell me. He was now a lecturer in anthropology at the City College of San Francisco, a teaching position he enjoyed, in a subject that fired his passion. His charm and wit were undiminished. In fact, his move to California seemed to have liberated him even further. He was a leader in the Latino wing of the gay rights movement and just as comfortable with himself as a gay man as he had been in New York. His taste was now almost exclusively Latino. He hung out at Esta Noche, a Latin bar in the Mission District and took home a new trick every night. We discussed his adventures in clinical detail when we met.

Pablo was the product of blue-collar parents, who had emigrated to the United States from Puerto Rico when he was just a child. While their constructed Spanish lineage allowed them to project the illusion of a superior heritage, the harsh reality of their tenement house testified to their true status on the mainland. Pablo's brother had been shot dead just yards from their front door, and Pablo's sister had her first abortion at thirteen, before eloping with a Chinese chiropractor. Her family had disowned her and had persuaded the Catholic Church to excommunicate her by virtue of her conversion to Buddhism. They had borne these series of tragedies with a show of great dignity.

Pablo's parents were sad and somewhat pathetic in their pride and took solace in the fact that their one remaining son was intelligent, academic, and seemed destined for a bright future. They had focused their attention on Pablo, instilling in him the family virtues of their past, and extolling him to make them happy by catalyzing the emancipation of the family from this morass of despair.

His admission to Columbia University brought great pride to them. His success with his undergraduate studies further cemented his status. Then one day his mother visited his dormitory room unannounced and found him in bed, naked with a man.

Pablo reacted to this discovery in an unexpected way. Rather than apologize for his sinful homosexuality, he "came out of the closet" overnight, without shame or fear. His first act was to take his boyfriend, Eric, a PH.D. student in engineering, home to his parents. He patiently sat with his parents through their anguish and recrimination, his mother's weeping and lamenting as her lovingly crafted vision for the family's future crumbled. Surprisingly, his father reacted with calm, even as his mother screeched and moaned, blaming herself, Pablo, Eric, the hormones his father had seeded her with through his sperm, and finally fate. This God-fearing and elegant woman finally recognized that Pablo was not going to change, that he would bed only men, and that he would not bear her grandchildren. Her adjustment was surprisingly swift, though she never formally acknowledged her son's homosexuality.

Pablo also "came out" at the university with a vengeance. He was a student leader in gay and Latino clubs. In classroom discussions, he would bring up gay liberation issues whenever possible. He walked with his then-current boyfriend through the university, hand in hand, turning a deaf ear to derogatory epithets. When called "fag," his typical response was: "Yes, honey, come and get it!" He was unapologetic, unrepentant, good-humored, and lively. If he had a serious side, he did not show it easily. Overall, Pablo was excellent company, and meeting him in San Francisco was a stroke of good luck.

Pablo and I spent evenings together from time to time, and on weekends he would host a communal brunch that included several recent tricks, friends, loud music, and much good fun. As a blow against "the cultural imperialism of the decadent West," his lovers were all Latino or black. He lived in San Francisco's predominantly Latino Mission District, where he introduced me to several men for casual sex, and I learned to appreciate the seductive and sensuous Latin temperament. I was quite enamored with the uninhibited romance that Latinos brought to sex, no matter how transient. My sexual life was filled with adventure, with beautiful young men with smooth, brown skin. Unlike many of the Pakistanis I had known, the generally hairless bodies were well proportioned, finely muscled. They also had fewer sexual inhibitions. Under Pablo's influence, I quickly became a "bean queen," as he called it. For the most part, my partners were generally empty-headed twinkies with beautiful bodies but no potential for a relationship. Their interest was limited to sex, dancing, and drinking.

While this was fun, I was unable to forge any lasting connection or to enter the community. Pablo and I lamented on occasion at the superficiality of California and reminisced about the intensity of New York and its men and the deep conversations and connections that now seemed impossible in a city that was always so disgustingly beautiful. While I was looking for greater depth, Pablo seemed quite content with his transient lifestyle. I was ready for love while, for Pablo, play seemed more than sufficient a basis for contentment.

Just as my life seemed stuck in this now monotonous routine, fate dealt an unlikely card. A Pakistani friend from Toronto announced plans to visit. Pablo offered to lend me his sleeping bag.

"I have a visitor from Colombia staying at my place," he said. "A shy kid that I've yet to break in. I'll let him know that you'll be over to pick up the sleeping bag."

This was how I first met Juan, at Pablo's apartment. He opened the door and, at first glance, I felt a familiar stirring in my loins. He smiled and introduced himself.

"Pablo told me you'd stop by," he said, retrieving the sleeping bag.

I introduced myself. We looked at each other for an uncomfortably long time. My interest in him must have been evident.

"So, how long are you visiting, Juan?"

"Oh, I'm moving here. I have a job offer as a programmer for an insurance company, and Pablo is letting me stay here until I find an apartment. I really like San Francisco. Where do you live?"

"Not very far away.... Would you like to come and visit me?"

"Sure."

On the way over to my apartment, he told me about his family. His father was an engineer in Bogotá, and he had seven brothers and sisters. He had come to the United States to visit, but had stayed because he liked it. He had told his family of his intention not to return, and they had not pressured him to go back so far. He had told them that he planned to finish college in the United States, though he was twenty-five.

We reached my apartment and I ushered him in. Once in private, we naturally moved closer. Almost in unison, we kissed, gently starting the process of lovemaking, in no hurry to move too quickly. It was almost as though we knew that this was just the first of many times. Gradually, we moved to the bed, and I soon knew that Juan was no ordinary trick: I had fallen in love. Being with Juan just felt . . . different.

Juan was charming, romantic, energetic, expressive, attentive, and affectionate. He was slightly shorter than me, slim and well proportioned, with smooth, brown skin and a brilliant smile. His wide dark-brown eyes flashed with feeling, and his boyish exuberance was infectious. With him I felt younger, and he created a sense of excitement and adventure in everything we did. I grew deeply attached to him. The phrase "I love you" came easily to him, and coming from him, these were the sweetest words to me. But I was not ready to repeat them, though I wanted only to be with him.

Within a few days he found an apartment, a seedy cubicle in the Mission, the best he could afford. He decorated it with style, and his little place became warm and cozy. I found myself spending a great deal of time there.

"Oh come on," Pablo teased weeks later. "I think you must be in love. You should be careful about such things! Love is a dangerous disease, if it prevents you from experiencing other men!"

Pablo was right. Within weeks, I had asked Juan to move in with me and he accepted. I extended my stay in San Francisco, in large part to be with Juan. He quickly occupied my apartment and made it his. As would a good Pakistani wife, he kept the apartment spotless, loved to shop, and took care of my needs before his own. Like a good Pakistani husband, I discreetly paid the bills, complaining only occasionally.

Before I knew it, we were "settled." We developed a social circle, consisting primarily of other couples. There was Jose and

Ariel, the giggly pair from Mexico to whom Juan was close. They had been together over five years in what clearly qualified as a long-term relationship. They would come over for long visits, Ariel's cousin Gabriel in tow, and the four would spend hours gossiping in Spanish and cooking delicious meals. Jose was a waiter, Ariel worked in a retail shop, and Gabriel was a student.

Our more professional friends included Bart and Ben, who had been together almost a decade. Ben, who was Chilean, was an engineer, and Bart, a computer product planner. We formed a close relationship with them; I got along well with Bart, and Juan with Ben. Weekends were spent camping out or simply camping it up at the Russian River. In all, our immediate circle consisted of perhaps a dozen friends. Juan had the social energy to keep the momentum of any party going and was the social manager of the house. We struck a good balance.

Juan's job situation had always been a bit tenuous, since new immigration laws promised to apply more stringent visa requirements for employment. Less than six months after we moved in together, these new laws took effect, and he lost his job. This was what he had feared, and I assured him that there was nothing to worry about and to take his time. In my way of thinking, this was just a glitch in our long-term relationship. No matter, I had a good job and was able to pay the bills. We were, I assured myself, looking at the long term, and this was just a temporary problem. He had already filed for immigration, and his visa would come through shortly, he assured me. From experience, I knew that these things took time. I assured him of my support, and he assured me in turn that our relationship was forever as far as he was concerned.

We considered plans for a future that in my mind had no horizon. Perhaps we would move into a house together on one of the hills in San Francisco, with views of the city. We dreamed about how we would decorate our house. We even went to real-estate open houses to see what we could afford once we were both working. We talked at length about how our life together would develop, once the immigration hurdle was past. We would travel to Pakistan and Colombia.

"Watch out," cautioned Pablo one day. "I think you are deeply in love. I don't think Juan is quite as deeply committed as you think. I know him well. Please don't take this badly, but I think he is using you. I think you are in love with love!"

I sniffed and dismissed such warnings, content for the first time with being gay and happy in my love for Juan. What did Pablo know about relationships, after all? He had not had one yet that lasted longer than a few weeks!

Juan had first come to the United States on a student visa from Colombia. He had had an upper-middle-class upbringing and displayed confidence and calm assurance. But out of seven siblings, he was the only one without a college degree. He had been a poor student and had dropped out of school at age sixteen. He had found a job and moved out of his parent's house to be independent. Despite a series of early girlfriends, he had always known that he was gay. At twenty-one, he attended night classes to finish his high school diploma. At twenty-four, he persuaded his father that he needed to get his degree in the U.S., applied and was accepted by a C-grade college and left with no intention of returning.

When we met, he was confronting the difficulties he faced in the U.S., alone and without his family status and prestige to support him. In retrospect, I should have recognized that I was a steppingstone for his goals. At that time, though, it seemed the dimensions of our love promised to span a lifetime. He worked hard to keep me happy and, to me, this meant that he was as interested in building for the long term as I was. In my mind, we were "married" in the Pakistani model, and we would take care of each other. He played the part of "wife" with fidelity and dedication and, in my mind, I added the dimension of longevity.

Juan and I had now been together for over two years. My apartment resembled a home, rather than the "crashpad" in Toronto that Nusrat had never quite succeeded in taming. It was attractively furnished, and there was always food in the refrigerator. Friends came over for dinner, and we had occasional parties. We spent weekends at the Russian River, a popular gay resort north of San Francisco, where we stayed and brunched in "gay" style. Juan bought fresh flowers every week and kept the house spotless. He systematically added to his wardrobe (and, occasionally, to mine)—tastefully colored Polo shirts and Ralph Lauren blue jeans. He was always well color-coordinated, and I was pleased that he took an interest in his appearance. I could show him off with pleasure and pride to my friends. As with the stereotypical straight relationship, he coordinated our home life, and I went to work.

I was indeed intoxicated with love, and Juan was the center of my non-work universe. His interests were somewhat limited, though. He did not read and had little use for music, art, or culture, except in its current and most vulgar forms. He was not an original thinker and felt that brand names, whether on clothes or opinions, were an adequate endorsement. Still, I was captivated much of the time I spent with him; not by his wit or wisdom, but by his charm, devotion, and stated willingness to forge a lifelong bond with me. The compromises I made were thus short-term sacrifices, needed to consolidate a position for the long term. I was happy.

We had a joint account for expenses, and I was the sole contributor to this account. He was thrifty at times, a good negotiator for services, and a comparison shopper. I could never say "no" to any of his requests, and he tailored his needs to be relatively reasonable, within the means of my paycheck. We certainly bought much more than I would have on my own, but I was a willing traditional male breadwinner, turning over his paycheck to a wife.

Our common relationships began to take on the flavor of his interests. My more intellectual friends receded into the background. We had parties and dinners, and the focus seemed to be on fun, laughter, and new experience. Our new friends compared notes on trips taken, men admired, purchases of clothes, furniture, and decorations. My books were packed in boxes and relegated to storage, replaced by decoration and design. This made Juan happy, so I was content.

Finally, Juan's visa petition came through. He had successfully obtained his green card, and was able to seek employment. More important for him, he was now able to travel. Through his outgoing charm and skill at networking, he had already received a verbal job offer. He could start whenever he was ready.

"We must travel while we can, and before I have to start my job," he said excitedly. "Why don't you take a month off from work, and let us have a good time."

I agreed and negotiated a month off.

We traveled to Europe. London was our first stop, followed by Paris, Madrid, then Switzerland. We flew between these cities, then rented cars or took trains. We stayed in executive-class hotels and meticulously saw all the sights. Where there was a compromise to be considered because of the expense involved, we generally opted to spend the money.

"Who knows when we will be back here next?" Juan reasoned. "Might as well do it now."

Gradually, I noticed a change in Juan's perspective as he discussed with me his return to the work force. His sentences, previously always couched in the familial "we" had now increasingly become "I." He was less effusive in his affection and on occasion a bit distant. I assumed that this was due to his anxiety about returning to work. I brought up the subject of moving to a larger apartment, perhaps even buying a house together, something he had always wanted, but he seemed less interested now.

"Let's wait and see," he would say.

Near the end of our trip, he became moody and, after our return home, was quite short-tempered and bitchy.

Once he started working, he would come home late. He was socializing with friends from work, he explained. I noticed that he did not volunteer to contribute to the joint account we had established for common expenses; his paycheck went into his own account. However, I did not think much about it. "Let him feel safe and secure with his own money," I thought.

Our relationship had changed, albeit gradually. Then one day, he brought up the issue of closed versus open relationships.

"I really love you, you know," he said, "and I know that you love me. But how would you feel if I met someone and brought him home? You know, just for fun. After all, it would not be like the two of us—this would just be casual. Maybe we can even have a threesome." He laughed.

Sickened, I told him it would be up to him whether he wanted to see other people, but that I felt that a monogamous relationship was fine for me.

"You can take them elsewhere," I added. "Do what you want, as long as they never set foot in our house. Also, I don't want to know about it or even discuss the subject."

We switched subjects. With charming ease, Juan started to discuss weekend plans as though nothing significant had happened. Tense and eager to change the subject myself, I persuaded myself that the moment had passed, that this had been a test lovers sometimes administer to their beloved. I pretended I had passed the exam.

But I had deceived myself.

One evening I returned early from a business trip to find that the door to the guest bedroom was shut, though the lights were on elsewhere in the house. Calling Juan's name, I knocked on the door and opened it.

They were in bed together. Sitting up, sheets to their waists, their torsos unclothed. He was a big, red-haired man. He looked as shocked as I felt. Juan had a strange smile on his face.

Too stunned to speak and too polite to raise an instant fuss in front of a stranger, I looked at them for a moment more, then numbly shut the door. I did not slam it.

Like a zombie, I walked out of the house, struggling to contain the tears that rolled down my face, the molten excreta of love exiting painfully, blinding me. As I tried to start the car, I was trembling in anguish, frozen in a state of shock. All I wanted was to get away from the now-defiled home that Juan and I had built together.

I drove aimlessly through the streets, alternately weeping and feeling calm, feeling lost and strangely detached.

Why did he have to bring another man home? Why did he not just leave, and come back to me when he felt ready? Was this calculated cruelty on his part, or did he simply lack feelings for me? If he lacked feelings, why had we been together so long? If this had been a practical arrangement for him, why had I vested so much of my soul in this bargain? Like a child, I had trusted him. Was this his betrayal, or my naïveté?

Was I so easily disposable? Was he really so uncompassionate? Was I angry, weary, sad, or just confused? We could have resolved this within the "family" he and I had created, couldn't we? That we were family counted, didn't it?

My head pounded from the circular thoughts tormenting me and waves of emotion that engulfed me.

An hour later, I found myself near Bart and Ben's home and called them from a pay phone. Bart answered.

"Hello, Bart. Am I disturbing you?"

"No, I'm just doing the dishes. Ben's not here."

"Do you mind if I come over?"

"Not at all, Badruddin. . . . Are you okay?"

"I'm okay," I hesitated. I didn't want to talk on the phone. "I'm nearby. I'll be there in a few minutes."

When he opened the door, Bart gave a critical glance and I knew my condition was obvious. He asked, sharply alarmed, "What's wrong?"

"Nothing," I replied, as he led me to the living room, giving me my moment to remain in control. When I sat on the sofa, trying to figure out what to say without sobbing, he asked me again, "Are you sure you're all right?"

No. Nothing is all right. The dam burst, and I wept uncontrollably. It was several minutes before I could speak and tell him what had happened. When I did, I narrated the events with a strange detachment. It was almost as if this were a story about someone else.

"What nerve!" remarked Bart when I had finished. He was livid. "What a terrible thing to do to you, after all you've done for him. He's such a goddamn fool. I can't stand to see him hurt you like this, Badruddin."

There was a long pause, as if Bart was biting his tongue, fighting his impulse to give me advice. "What will you do?"

"I don't know. What would you do?"

"I'd kick his ass out."

But I couldn't bring myself to anger as quickly as Bart had. I could not go back and tell him to leave immediately. Juan was my family, we had been through difficult and fun times together, and we had planned for the long term. This was just a glitch, I told myself, we will work together to resolve this.

"I thought I had made it clear that he could do as he wished, but not in our house."

"The nerve . . ."

"But all our years together count for something, don't they? Or does this mean he thinks we're over?"

"I don't know what's in his mind, Badruddin."

"I think we simply need to discuss this. Perhaps we can salvage our home."

"Perhaps."

"All relationships change and there are challenges."

"But sometimes people outgrow their relationships, Badruddin."

"Yes, but if we can talk reasonably, we'll understand each other better. I'm not unreasonable about his bringing men to our house, am I?"

"Of course not. It is your home."

"Well, then, perhaps he is just testing me. Perhaps this is a test to see if I really love him?"

"Honey, he's shitting on you."

"Yes. This he will never do again. I will make that clear. Once he understands my point of view, he will accept. We will forgive, forget, and move on."

As I left, Bart embraced me and said, "Please let me know if there is anything we can do. If you need a place to stay while you both sort things out, you are absolutely welcome here. I hope you know that."

Calmer, and even hopeful, but still tense, I returned home. Juan was sitting on the sofa, watching TV and drinking a Tequila Sunrise. I stood there waiting for him to speak. He took a deep drink, flicked off the TV using the remote, and turned his scowling face toward me.

"What was that all about? Since when do you barge into closed rooms like that? And then leave without saying anything. I am really pissed off!"

Bewildered, I started to calmly try to explain to him what the problem was. "*Our home . . . our home . . . our home . . .*" He had expertly put me on the defensive.

"Yes, this is *my* home also, and who I want to bring here when you are not here is my business. We already talked about this."

There was a long brutal silence. "Listen," he finally said, in a more conciliatory tone. "I don't want to hurt you, like I said, but I want to see other people as well. You should have called if you were coming back early. It is not my fault. So, I brought him here, what's wrong with that? You were not supposed to be here. You just show up, barge in on something guys do all the time. It's no big deal. It was just this guy visiting from Texas. I picked him up at Macy's. He's leaving tomorrow. And I won't see him again anyway. You really freaked him out, and that's not fair. Why don't you just relax a bit, nothing has really changed, don't be so uptight! Look, we can set up a system so that we let each other know in advance, so that such a thing does not happen again."

Juan had deftly turned this into my problem. But though he might win points for his position in argument, his cuckolding of me and his ruthlessly unapologetic response tore at my heart.

There was no point showing my feelings to him, no point trying to reason with him. It was clear that we were beyond that.

"I am sorry, but I can't handle this," I muttered. "We cannot live together under these circumstances."

Alarmed, Juan moved closer to me, and smiled assuringly. "Look, don't overreact. Relax. I am sorry, but we can work this out as part of our living arrangement, okay? I could move into the guest bedroom, and that will solve the matter, right? Let's become like roommates."

My head wanted him to stay, but my heart wanted him to leave, and perhaps for the first time ever in my life, my heart won over my head. In my head, I saw us working things out practically, sharing costs to stay together at the beautiful home we had created together. *I loved him so deeply, I could hide this,* my head reasoned. *At least he would be around me while I pretended to feel just friendship. If he was not my lover anymore, so be it—we had so much invested so much in each other, why waste it? Let him stay. You know each other so well. Become friends. You can also find someone new. He has a sensible solution, let him stay.*

My heart knew otherwise. It was in pain and refused to stay in its usual silent subservience. *I am in agony,* it seemed to say, *and so long as Juan is around this will not change. I cannot let him go just because you will it. Someone new? You are in fantasyland if you believe that you will give anyone new a fair chance if he continues to stay here. You love him, and he obviously does not love you. You will be chained to the futile hope that he will love you once again. He will manipulate your love for him to his advantage, and you will be sorry. Get as far away from him as possible, so that you can swallow the bitter pill of separation and start to heal. Just roommates?*

"No," I finally answered. "Either this never happens again, or you must leave. I want your answer right now."

Even as his cutting words tumbled out, I wanted Juan to recant his decision, rewind the scenario we were in, tell me it had all been a nightmare. Please, I silently begged him, please. I love you, and this is the first time I have really ever loved anyone. Do not do this to me. If you must do it, be charitable and find a way that is less painful to me. Don't be so ruthless. But it was not to be.

Now Juan showed a new face, practical and efficient. He would leave as soon as he could, he told me. However, he would need help with the deposit to a new apartment. He would, of course, need things for his new place from the kitchen, and he asked if he could take his pick from the momentos from our trips together? Too numb to argue and too astonished by his instant switch from romantic to practical, I assented without argument to what he asked. There was little emotion in his demeanor, which was cold. It was obvious that I had already become part of his history. Within a week he had gone, loaded with things from the house, and our relationship was reduced to occasional calls about mail that had not been forwarded.

I discovered afterwards that his big red-headed Texan actually lived nearby, and that Juan had moved in with him.

☙ ❧

"You know about a year ago Juan told Ben about all these tricks Juan had," Bart told me one evening. "But Juan said that you had agreed to an open relationship. Knowing you, I doubted this, but it is never wise to get involved in people's private lives, no matter how close we are. Now it is over and you can find someone who deserves you. Ben says to leave you alone, but I know a few single guys you might want to date. You just let me know, and I'll arrange it for you."

☙ ❧

"I told you, but you would not listen," lectured Pablo. "Juan always saw his relationship with you as temporary while he was getting settled. You should not be so surprised. I tried to tell you so many times, but your mind was closed. You have to be careful with relationships where money is a factor. Also, I understand the Latin temperament. When I talked with him, it was always clear that his real feelings were for himself. I think you got used. Learn a lesson, and move on.

"Listen, how about a hot date? There is this really cute Puerto Rican I can introduce you to. . . ."

Though I appreciated Bart's and Pablo's offers, they were premature. My relationship with Juan left me emotionally scarred, and it would be some years before I could even consider a new partner, let alone go on a date with a goal other than just sex. I had invested heavily in my relationship with Juan and, as time passed, I asked myself whether I had truly believed that our relationship would last, given all the differences between us. In retrospect, the writing on the wall was clear to everyone but me, who should have seen it all along.

I discovered later that Juan had broken up with his new lover. The Texan had left him for a younger, even better-looking Mexican boy. Through mutual friends, I heard that Juan had expressed fond memories of our time together, and had expressed regrets about leaving. He used intermediaries to see if I was interested in accepting him back. Too late! He was now in the past, a chapter already written. It was time to move on.

Eventually I had no regrets, since Juan had shown me that "love," however illusory, was possible between men. My first love had broken my heart, but he had also shown me that I had a heart and that it could heal.

The Taste Of Love

Juan's departure from my life was a mixed blessing. On the one hand, I had to somewhat sheepishly acknowledge that I had been totally blind to his intentions. Several friends had pointed out to me that, while Juan and I were together, there was a mismatch between us at several levels. He was undereducated, materialistic, and financially dependent on me. Perhaps I had subconsciously understood this and felt that his dependency would keep him in the relationship. As in a male-chauvinistic heterosexual marriage where the house-enslaved wife has nowhere to go, perhaps my insecurity prevailed with Juan. Perhaps, I reasoned with myself, I should seek a balanced, equal relationship that is validated daily.

Juan's departure drove me to self-doubt. As a Muslim and Pakistani, a "family," of whatever ilk, was central to my nesting instinct. And yet, without the prospect of children and without any hope of integration within the extended family environment, what hope could there be? Was there a brand of permanence that I could strive for in a relationship with another man? Or was I destined to be alone forever, except for temporary arrangements? Did Juan typify the best gay life had to offer? Was I culturally preprogrammed to find a "wife" I could dominate, making a truly egalitarian relationship out of the question? Would the only relationship I could accept be akin to the one I had with Juan, containing within it seeds of its own destruction?

Over the years I had consciously distanced myself from my parents and siblings, once it was clear that I would not grow the family organism through procreation. Was it time for me to reattach myself and attempt remarriage? Or should I plan to remain single, becoming an aging "uncle" figure to my family and friends, one who was doomed to settle for clandestine sexual episodes instead of the relationship I wanted?

Despite my self-doubts, I was left with an exhilarating sense that I had been through one relationship and this meant that another could be possible. I had felt "love"—whatever I might label it later—for another man, which was not rooted entirely in sex. I had proven my capacity to express my emotional feelings for another man, and we had lived together. True, the relationship was flawed. Equally true, it did not last very long. But this was California, where the half-life of an average relationship, straight or gay, was often measured in weeks and months. By living with Juan, I had for the first time demonstrated the meaning of the word "gay," as it applied to me. By associating with our friends through our social activities together, I had experienced a sense of a gay community. And by working together to create a home, I had experimented with the notion of family, in a gay context. Long averse to labels and classifications, I had to admit to myself that I was, perhaps, indeed, gay. The most delightful part of this self-discovery was that it was a very natural to me. I felt at home when I roamed the Castro. I felt with "family" when I cruised the bars in the Mission with Pablo.

I had finally come of age. Far along already in my life, I was only now starting to fashion a true identity. Playing with the tailor's penis twenty years ago was curiosity. Experimenting in Mykonos was adventure. Driving Greg's "Cadillac" was pleasure. Those were events that were ultimately unconnected to what I now perceived as my core reality. During the early period of my life, my overarching concern was to follow the plan laid out for me: get married, raise a family, be a good and dutiful son. Juan had raised the possibility, kindled the hope, that I might someday be able to find a loving partnership with a man that would endure.

My experience with Juan had also allowed me to dare to reveal myself where previously my life had been totally hidden. I had introduced him to close friends who were straight. Some of these first introductions were made in trepidation and in great fear.

I had introduced Juan to John, a school friend from Columbia days who was well settled with three children and a wife. In the past, he had asked me about my marriage, sympathized about the breakup, and had tried to set me up with various women.

"Living alone like that in San Francisco is not a safe thing to do," he had joked. "You should be dating. You would make some poor San Francisco girl very happy."

I had mumbled something about being busy at work, having family issues, and so on, and managed to maintain a social relationship with John and his wife Linda over the years.

When John and Linda eventually met Juan, I was the only person in the room who was tense. They became instant friends, and without my saying a word, they understood where Juan fit into my life.

"So how long have you guys been together?" asked Linda, and there was nothing more to say. It was the most natural thing in the world. It instantly validated our relationship and made my life seem normal.

One of the enduring legacies of my relationship with Juan was that it laid out an alternative, skeletal blueprint to my life. While with Juan, I led two distinct lives: one personal and one professional. Everyone else at work had a visible personal life. I did not. But my personal life had its own domain in which my work life was rarely discussed. With Juan's friends, and the common friends we attracted, there was little interest in my professional life. If there was interest, I felt compelled to be less than forthcoming, to avoid the risk of being revealed as gay within my professional network. This was a cost I was not willing to incur, since the benefit of being "out," if any, had not been readily apparent. Secrecy, it seemed, was a small price to pay in a homophobic society where one's alternatives in life could be unnecessarily restricted. I was accustomed to this burden, and would shed it in a managed way over time. One of the unintended benefits of my relationship with Juan was that there was now a real benefit to "coming out" to people. I now had something to share with them, something to say about myself. Without Juan as living proof, there had been nothing to say, and no valid reason to "come out."

Besides making me aware of how closely the question of coming out was related to my having a love relationship, Juan's departure also raised another question: What was my "type" of man and was this an important consideration for me in searching for a potential partner? Was I looking in all the wrong places for the wrong type of person? Was I searching properly, or simply accepting what came along? How does one look for a partner in the gay world?

Closets vs. "Mr. Right"

My relationships with men were all accidental. I met them casually and had relationships of varying duration. There is today no mainstream social-support system in North America to help men develop relationships. No matchmakers, no tea parties, no investigation into family background, and no vetting of prospective partners by friends. Almost always, relationships are fired by lust. Just as predictably, many fail when that fire subsides. The majority of my sexual contacts with men were casual, which meant that I would have sex one or more times, and then disengage. While an element of adventure may have made such contacts appealing on their own merits, I would have long ago settled into a pleasant relationship with a male partner if I had found the right person, and would have gladly focused my energy elsewhere.

It is true that straight couples are also required to find their own partners in North America. The process, however, is dramatically different, with families, social networks, and friends mobilizing to action to welcome or criticize the potential partner. There are parties at work to celebrate the union. The pair make a simple and easily understood public statement of their relationship through words and by simply being together. They are acknowledged to be married, or they are dating. Everybody can know. There is nothing to hide, and there is nothing to explain. There is also no need to discuss and decide how the married couple will operate: if the man works and the woman stays home, he is not seen as a "sugar daddy." Top or bottom roles are relatively fixed. There are no guest lists to be edited, no separate communities to cultivate.

All this seemed necessary to me in a gay relationship. For many of my friends, the decision to "come out" seemed an easy choice, but it was not so clear-cut for me. What does it mean to be "gay?" In the culture of my birth, simply having sex with a man was no reason to make announcements about one's innermost identity. If I acknowledged my same-sex affectional preference, should I use the word "gay," and simply dismiss those who don't understand and harbor stereotypes? Should I be unconcerned if they acted on their stereotypes and denied me full access to society and its opportunities? Or should I care? The secret hardly seemed a burden after a lifetime of experience. In fact, no one asks. In that case, why tell?

I acquired my wife Nusrat through an arrangement that incorporated my family background and values. Like an employment agreement, it was based on the reasonable assumption that, while transient attributes such as her physical appeal were important, in the long term what would count were her root values. These values included a sense of family history and social obligation, a commitment to make the marriage work despite my eccentricities, if any, and to build a family with children. These shared values were what would make the match successful in the long run and smooth over any bumps along the way. Since our destiny as a family was either to raise children or remain pitifully childless, our personal satisfaction with each other was incidental to the overall social good of extending the family. It would be wonderful if we loved each other, nice indeed if we could tolerate each other over succeeding decades, and sad, but not fatal, to the marriage if we actively disliked each other and stayed together for the sake of family—not just children, but the extended family and its reputation.

Underlying this social contract are the edicts of Islam, which require men to marry and to extend the community by bearing children. The extended family, the tribe, and the *ummah* also required this. The social framework is represented in the punishment to be meted out to those who stray. As the Quran *Shareef* says:

> If any of your women is guilty of an immoral act, bring four of your men to give evidence; if they testify against them, retain them in the houses until death, or until God provides some other way for them. If two among you are guilty of such acts then punish both of them. But if they repent and reform, let them be, for God accepts repentance and is merciful.

Women are special, since their immorality carries with it the potential mark of maternity. Men, on the other hand, can have only trivial relationships with each other, and these are not serious enough for them to be locked away from society.

Contemporary Christianity seems to regard homosexuality as a grave sin, far worse than adultery or fornication without marriage. It may be naughty for a man and a woman to have carnal intercourse outside marriage, but for two men to engage in sex seems to provoke moral horror and distaste. Islam, however, focuses less on the act than the consequences. Two men consorting in private can hardly shake society, hence they should be warned and let off without punishment.

Paradoxically, this view does not recommend Islam to homosexuals. Christianity may be interpreted as condemning and censuring sex between men as unnatural and inherently evil, but it at least grants such interchange the stature of sin. Since homosexuality is sinful, it has a role in the morality play of heaven and hell. Marked as sinful, homosexuals can be burnt, condemned, redeemed, or reformed. To be so marked, they must have an identity to struggle against, to be marked by, and to be liberated through. As the Shudras of the Hindu caste system are marked by birth, so are homosexuals defamed by their desires and marked by their "unnatural" actions in the Christian West. The struggle against condemnation also helps to create the underground movement that can foster an alternative identity. It is perhaps not surprising that gay liberation movements have started in the Christian West, where the "Shudras" of society have clamored for recognition, flaunted their difference, flouted convention, and seized sufficient social power to speak of liberation. There is a battle of "right" versus "wrong," the Christian right versus the liberals, "bad" versus "good," "corruption" versus "righteousness," individual rights versus community values.

The lines are drawn, there is a call to battle in the war for the higher ground. The loser regroups for the next round, and slowly, inch by inch, there is progress, painfully slow, but progress nonetheless. And when the community stops momentarily to assess its advance, there is jubilation. We have moved far in advancing gay rights, not far enough by any means, but the road is wide open and the implements of battle are at hand. There is an excited sense of exhilaration with each little victory. From marches to new laws, from legal equality to gay marriage, each advance is thrilling.

Under Islam, there is no adversary. Men who have sex with men and are witnessed in this act by four adult men must repent. Repentance can be repeated as often as necessary and, in the absence of a moral label, maintaining privacy in such matters is usually the best course of action. There are good and persuasive reasons that men can use to explain their actions to themselves, if they feel that there is a need to reconcile what they do with what society expects. An unmarried man can justify sex with another man by blaming his unruly erection, pointing out that the alternative of sex with a female prostitute was financially unaffordable. A married man could castigate his natural sexual appetite for his dalliance with men, pointing out that to consort instead with a woman would be to humiliate his wife and family, waste family money, and run the risk of creating a child. Sexual desire is considered normal in mainstream Islam (there is no celibate order of mullahs, unlike Catholic priests), so such explanations are not even necessary and usually best left unsaid.

As a Muslim, "coming out" was for me more than just the recognition that I was gay. This was something I had known at some subconscious level since childhood, so it was not a big surprise. Rather, coming out is the act of becoming a distinct human being, separate from the community. Such a separation occurs naturally after high school in North America, but it may never occur in Pakistan. This has been the difficult part, and perhaps one day I will claim myself released.

My identity continues to develop on several levels. Who I am seems at times to be an artificial construct of the various communities I live in. To my colleagues at work, I am foreign-born, a rich cultural experience to some, and a "Paki" and a "wog" to others. To my Pakistani brethren, I am a somewhat distant community member who oddly is still single. To my gay friends, I am a "closet case." Chased by "curry queens"[1] and boxed in by labels, I am still mapping my identity.

I grew up in a culture where belonging was everything. Today I live in a stratum where individuality is prized. This should, on the face of it, provide me with unconstrained latitude to build a new life. However, this freedom to define myself anew is false liberty. While it is true that men in North America can separate work from family and live private lives as single individuals, such distinctions are unnatural to me. While I feel there is no shame or guilt associated with being gay, the strain of a segmented life is the cause of much stress. Life is a constant balance of lies and deceptions, half-truths and evasions.

John, a colleague at work, is a great "friend." He invites me to the informal get-together he is having this Friday evening at his house. Almost everyone from the group will drop by, with spouses. If spouses are unable to join, they will be referenced: "Sorry Carol could not make it, she had to pick up the kids." All those present have lives outside work and share some of these experiences with others. This meeting has an implicit purpose: to engender trust. These are the people

---

[1] A camp/pejorative gay slang phrase denoting predominant attraction to South Asian men.

I live with half my waking hours, yet have nothing to say to after the work is done. How can I relax with them?

"Sorry, I have a friend from out of town visiting and have to take him to dinner." I say.

"Really, where from?"

"New York."

"Sounds like fun! Family friend?"

"No, we used to work together, he is a consultant and is here on a project. This is the only evening he has open."

Lies, more lies.

Yes, I did meet Dick in New York. We met in the Bulldog Baths on 14th Street near the Village. Sex with him was sweet, but his smile was sweeter still, and now after such a long time he had written to me out of the blue. I am on my way, and I am filled with anticipation, remembering his body, his good humor, and his gentle affection.

What could I have said to my coworker: "Sorry John, an old trick is showing up tonight, can't make it to the party"?

Each little lie, each easy evasion encrusts the soul. Gay liberation advocates coming out completely, to get it over with whatever the cost, so that others can either accept you or to reject you. It tells us that it is better to die courageously on your feet than to cower in a closet.

I hear it said among fashionable gay circles that coming out is passé—why, everyone who is anyone has done it already. What a lie! Even men with partners hide out in corporate America in porous cocoons, gay ostriches who no one sees or acknowledges. For each Malcolm Forbes, Rock Hudson, and Liberace, there are thousands of less famous others who, like them, must also continue to live secret lives of solitary grief in order to make their contribution to our "open" society.

As a Muslim in North America, there is an additional closet: the closet of the Pakistani and Muslim communities. In this chatterbox world, friends and relatives halfway around the world are affected by innuendo and gossip. Because "gay" is a state of being that is unknown and unrecognized in Muslim Pakistan, it is derisively viewed as a manifestation of the decadent West. Am I *hijra*, or a *gandu*? Do I have a medical problem that prevents me from marrying and raising a family? What is wrong? The shame is social, not personal. The victim is not the individual, but the family. The family is cursed, its roots are tainted, its genetic soundness is questioned, the marriageability of others in the family is at issue, and the stakes are high: not simply individual angst, but tragedy on a grand scale.

My solution had been the selective sharing of my affectional orientation with people, and making it a point not to lie about it should someone ask. Without a partner there was little to say, and discussing one's practices in bed, or affectional preferences, seems in bad taste unless it is to make a political point. Juan and I had met some of my straight friends who hitherto had not known. When they met Juan, they knew, but after Juan and I broke up, nothing was discussed. There was nothing to say, and they would not be useful to me in finding a new partner. Better to focus on this goal, I reasoned, rather than invest needless energy in a coming-out program!

Looking forward, there seemed to be more questions than answers.

Family

I am living in a period in which the threat of AIDS is devastating large sections of the gay community. I have seen friends get sick and die from this dreaded and dreadful disease. In the midst of this anguish and tragedy, the communal liberation of gay men and lesbians has been gaining ground. For me to neither benefit from this liberation nor play some part in alleviating the suffering brought on by AIDS would be a personal tragedy.

I learned a great deal from the humanity of friends afflicted by this disease, and the compassion of those that cared for them. In the face of such life-and-death issues, my questions seemed minor, almost irrelevant.

I had become an avid practitioner of the gospel of safer sex, but sex was ultimately always unsafe. After Haider, I became much more cautious. I would get tested regularly. I could, and did, consistently prevent the interchange of bodily fluids with sexual partners, but I could not avoid exposing my heart to the sweet and very unsafe ravages of passion. The romantic Pakistani in me refused to become jaded, and to categorize sex as just another appetite.

The company that had moved me from Toronto to San Francisco later downsized. My job was eliminated, another bitter reality in these days of intense global competition. My business visa to work in the U.S.A. was no longer valid, and I would have to return home to Canada, or perhaps even back to Pakistan. I chose Toronto, carrying the bruises of one relatively major relationship, and several minor ones.

I was back home. What lay ahead?

I tried to look for a job in my field, but was frustrated with the choices available. My expertise is quite specialized. After several weeks of frustration, my old employer hired me on as a consultant. What irony! I was paid twice as much on an hourly basis for doing the same job.

With this transition from employee to consultant came a degree of independence. Being laid off was the best thing that happened to me professionally. Socially I slipped further away from the large and still-traditional Pakistani community in Toronto. In many cases, I simply did not renew ties that had been fragile from the start. Instead, I started to forge closer ties to the mainstream gay community in Toronto. My search for love could stop when I met a suitable man. But, who and how?

That was when my partner Dick entered the picture. After a hard day at work in my home office, I stopped by the neighborhood bar for a beer. It had been a warm day. This was not a gay bar, but my gaze drifted to a man at the other end of the bar. He was blond with Nordic features and a solid build. His blue eyes seemed to twinkle at me through the cigarette haze, his gaze was steady and his slight smile ambiguous. Weary, but feeling somewhat reckless, I slid off the bar stool and walked over, tankard in hand. Normally I would not have given him a second look, since my preference was always for ethnic men, Latin, Asian, or South European. Dick, however, seemed different.

"Hi," I said. He was about my height, smaller than he appeared from afar. His white skin was stretched over wide cheekbones, an angular nose was perched over a cleft chin. His chilled blue eyes gave me goose bumps, as they simultaneously flashed fire and ice.

"Hello," he said. "I'm Dick. Looks like we both enjoy Lablatt on tap." I wondered what else we had in common

As it turned out, we had little else in common, except for a fevered passion for each other's bodies in bed, and complementary personalities that helped us form a bond of mutual respect and a commitment that we both hoped would be durable. He was light skinned, blond, with wispy hair, a light beard, and a virtually hairless body, which was built like a smaller version of Michaelangelo's David. I am dark, with a heavy beard and dense body hair (except on my thinning scalp), and spindly South Asian legs supporting an expanding middle-age paunch.

Our relationship reflected our differences. He is moody and emotional. I am level-headed and practical. He is artistic and creative and takes joy in the beauty of nature and the arts. I take joy in his joy. We are complementary to the point of no competition; even in bed, he is a delighted and delightful bottom, yelling endearments as my pelvis pounds against the golden muscular orbs of his buttocks. He eats salads but learned to cook curry for me. I learned to give him the quiet time that he needs for introspection.

When he came over to me, kissed me and told me that he loved me, I knew he spoke from the heart. When he asked me if I loved him as well, my answer was in the affirmative. Was this true, and what did "love" mean to me? These answers were not to be discovered through investigation, but through living life. I found that the common view we shared of our future meant more than the differences in our past.

Eventually Dick moved in with me, and we progressed towards a more egalitarian relationship. I now cook for him from time to time. He has even introduced me to the pleasures of being an occasional bottom. He is laid back, relaxed, moody, and often stubborn. Steadily, he has worn away the intensity and manic focus that had hitherto permeated my life. Yes, perhaps this is indeed love.

My consulting occasionally took me abroad to Europe but Dick preferred to stay home. He did not enjoy traveling. While we understood our relationship to be monogamous, it was also implicitly assumed that when I was traveling I would occasionally take advantage of sexual opportunity. There was no guilt associated with this on my part; Muslim men are permitted transient sex partners when traveling away from their families, as long as they fulfill their obligations to their families. Monogamy is a practical consequence of living with a spouse at home. We did not discuss this, nor did I inquire about Dick's dalliances, if any. In a curious turn away from the brown and black bodies of Pablo, Juan, and Greg, I was now almost exclusively interested in Northern Europeans, the whiter the better. Even when traveling to Spain or Greece, I found that the white flesh turning red at the beach stirred my loins far more than the sandy brown natives. It may seem politically incorrect to some, but my tastes in sexual partners now favor the Nordic look, pallid white in dark brown, or, more typically, dark brown in white. Those who know me understand that this change of taste was definitely not a case of a member of an oppressed colored race reacting to deep subliminal memories of being colonized, and then using an interracial relationship to attain some measure of psychological relief. This was just another normal relationship.

Dick in Karachi

It was time to visit Pakistan again, and I persuaded Dick to join me. It had been five years since my last visit. Aurangzeb and I had lost contact. My parents had moved into semiretirement in Islamabad, where the climate was more agreeable and there was less urban chaos. My father found solace in the company of other retirees and my mother, always cheerful and sociable, enjoyed the round of parties and picnics.

Since I had business to conduct in Karachi, we stayed at the Sheraton Hotel, across from the Pearl Continental Hotel, and down the road from the U.S. Consulate. Dick and I shared a room, which had two beds, though it was clear to the staff that only one bed needed to be made up each morning. There was no comment.

On our arrival I called Aurangzeb, and he showed up the following day.

"I've canceled my appointments for the day. So delightful to see you back!" he boomed warmly. "We are going to have lunch at the Sind Club down the road, with a party later at night at my house. Just a few of my friends, you know." He wanted to show us around.

As we left, he sidled up to me and whispered, "Such a hunk," referring to Dick. "Must be hot! Hung like a donkey, is he?"

I laughed, delighted at Aurangzeb's libidinal predictability, but said nothing.

The Karachi "gay" social circuit left me cold. It was just as I had recalled, except these were now middle-aged men with families, wives, and children, discussing their latest boys. I found that I envied their comfortable, socially secure lives much less than I had in the past. As they leered at Dick, I found myself explaining that we were a couple and we lived together, and that our relationship was more than just romance and sex—it was all of life. It was not a comfortable life with servants and familial security, but a life full of hard choices, daily discipline, and constant labor to simply build a basic relationship. These friends seemed content, but they too had to work to maintain their living standards and social rankings. Aurangzeb still had his stable of "boys," men in their twenties, who he was now content to visit just once a week. His wife "knew" of his sexual tastes, but they never spoke of it. He was a good father, a good husband, and a good son. Nothing else needed to be said.

Aurangzeb arranged to have his driver pick us up from our hotel. As I approached his familiar house, I noticed that it had been expanded substantially. Aurangzeb and his immediate family had their own private wing, separate from his parents' section. Separated by a courtyard was Aurangzeb's private "office," which included a small bedroom and a small library; it had private access from the street. I could imagine how the bed was used. His office was spacious enough to accommodate the entire group. He had arranged for dinner to be brought in from the main house, so that our gathering could be completely private. There was a clear view of the courtyard, which made it easy to notice if someone from the main house was on their way over.

As we progressed beyond the jocular, I spoke about life in Toronto, about being gay, gay liberation, and the community there.

"I still don't know how you do it," said Aurangzeb. "I think in Karachi you have the best of both worlds."

Dick charmed the group with his frankness and good humor.

"We have to do everything ourselves," Dick laughed. "It must be wonderful to have servants do all the work, and then have sex readily available on the side. But, we are a couple, and we spend much of our time with other gay couples or simply going about our day-to-day routine. My parents had us over for Christmas and consider us to be part of the family. I guess it is a different feeling. Of course we sleep in the same bed, but romance seems to include dealing with Badruddin's snoring and his aromatic farts, particularly after a heavy curry dinner. I cook a number of Pakistani dishes quite well, you know. My chicken curry is the envy of Toronto."

Everyone laughed. There seemed to be a twinge of envy blended in with the obvious tranquil comfort of this crowd.

Some of the group were younger men in their early twenties, and they seemed more interested in the alternative arrangement that we were describing.

"I think you have a wonderful life," said Mobeen, a student at St. Patrick's, who had been intently listening to our discussion. "I would love to have a lover. I can't stand these lies and secrets we have to put up with over here. I want to live with a man. I want a man to be my lover. I wish we had some sort of a gay movement here."

There was an uncomfortable silence for a moment; we all knew this was not possible.

"But you see, Islam is a wonderful blend of the practical and the necessary," argued Daud who, like Aurangzeb, had made the necessary accommodations. "We need family and religion to keep everything in place, and then we can basically do what we want. This is freedom."

"But it is all hidden. You have to appear so conservative," Mobeen pouted.

"Yes, our society is conservative., but it has its advantages," Aurangzeb said. "For instance, there are a lot of horny men and, unless you're married, no available women." Everyone laughed.

Someone else commented: "This society is now becoming so materialistic. Boys won't come with you for love alone; you have to pay them with gifts or cash. Even then you have to be careful, some will even try to threaten you with exposure after sex, though such blackguards are easily handled. I have had bad experiences in recent years."

Daud nodded and said, "Even with these problems, I cannot see myself living in a place like Toronto or San Francisco, in a gay ghetto, with AIDS everywhere."

"Excuse me, but anyone can get AIDS, even here in Pakistan," Dick injected.

"Of course, and we have heard of some cases here. But most people think of it as a gay disease."

"Yes, another added. "The big problem is, when you take a boy you are taking your chances. You cannot use a condom, otherwise he thinks you are gay, so you have to go without. This is a bit of a problem, particularly with AIDS."

"So, you're willing to risk your life just so a man on the street you pick up doesn't think you're gay?" Dick said, a bit too incredulously.

There was an uncomfortable silence, until Daud spoke: "Well, the main advantage of living in Karachi for me, at least, is that when I grow old here I will have my family around me. How can you live so alone?"

"Well, I am not sure what Badruddin would say," said Dick. "I guess we are 'alone' in the way you see things, as far as biological family is concerned. But we have our own version of family—people we have, in a sense, adopted. I would say that they are just as much family as any other type of family. When our friend Jim was diagnosed with AIDS, everyone pitched in to help care for him. He was never alone. Isn't that what families are about? So, we don't really live alone. The difference is, our 'family' is adopted, and everyone knows we are gay. We can turn to each other for comfort and advice, without the need to hide anything. That is one advantage, I suppose. On the other hand, you are right, we do not have the family we grew up with. I guess it is a real tradeoff, after all."

We talked for a while longer. Dick spoke about his family, which included a lesbian cousin. They had marched together in New York's Gay Pride parade the year before, and she had come out to her parents shortly thereafter. He described our routine at home in Toronto and some of our friends, who are mostly professional. Aurangzeb and his friends listened politely, asking questions. They asked about baths and bars in Toronto, and where they should visit on their next international jaunt. Dick was enjoying the discussion and was the center of attention, a diamond set off by curious brown faces scrutinizing him.

As the conversation continued, I began to understand that I was no longer part of this circle. Somewhat sadly, I realized that I could not return home again. The essential pieces of the game were different. I was no longer adept at playing it and not particularly interested. Yet I feared even in Toronto I would have to live alone, and, probably, die alone as well, far away from my homeland. Relationships formed through romantic love could be so transient, so unlike the permanence of family. A sobering thought.

Dick found the meeting to be fascinating and the rest of his trip to Pakistan to be a lot of fun. He was the main attraction wherever he went, whether at social gatherings or in the bazaar. The showman in him loved this attention, and he played his role as foreigner with gusto.

☙ ❧

We returned home to Toronto, exhausted but ready to restart our lives.

The search for love and meaning is also a process of self-discovery, and since that time I have been making slow, but steady, progress in this area with Dick and with myself. Looking forward, it is increasingly important to me that my future integrate the different parts of life: love, work, and community. Now, in middle-age, I see younger gay people starting to build their lives with greater confidence, with reasonable expectations for future happiness.

South Asian gay groups have emerged. I see the crucial role of politics and social activism in energizing the gay community, as well as creating power for gays in the mainstream.

Perhaps most importantly, I realize that I am unequivocally gay and am willing to stand up and be counted. I have slipped out of the closet, walking sideways. I have introduced Dick to straight friends and coworkers in Canada and the United States, but not my family. I walk in gay pride parades, though I still take pains to try to blend in invisibly with the group, rather than be the one who carries the banner. My new career as a business consultant has given me more time and opportunity to socialize and pursue other interests.

My closet door is open, though when necessary I can slip back in. This is certainly true when I visit Pakistan, though I have not been back since Dick and I were there together. In my homeland there is no meaning to my sexual orientation, or the word "gay." Exposing my gayness would be of no benefit to me in Pakistan; it could even entail tremendous social costs. The specter of AIDS continues to be associated with being gay, and I have no wish to tarnish my family's reputation on a principal.

When Dick and I traveled to Pakistan, I introduced him as a friend, though we shared a hotel room. I know speculation abounds that he may be my lover, though no one raised the subject.

It seems that I am destined to spend my final days far away from my geographic origins, and my cultural and religious foundation. I find that I am also distant from other Pakistanis and Muslims in Toronto. These are my choices, and I am content with them. Despite the many years I have been away, the culture of my birth still shapes how I look at things and my expectations from life; however, I face the future with enthusiasm and hope. Dick and I are considering a "marriage" ceremony, which would unite us in a formal domestic partnership. How will I introduce him in Pakistan after we are married?

Outside Toronto is the bedroom community of East York, a quiet, pleasant city with broad streets and single-family houses. We live on a cul-de-sac, and our bedroom faces the road. It is a small house, but large enough for our needs. The garden sports flowers in the spring, and when the weather turns warm, a light aroma floats in the air. I stand in the garden in the evening with my eyes closed, nose twitching, senses focused on the smell. My memories of the rich and sweet smell of *raat ki raani* return, but in the quiet and isolated patch of land we occupy, that special scent seems far away, a distant thought, a forgotten feeling. There is no chirping of birds, and no traffic noise. All is silent.

Dick calls me to dinner, and I go inside our cozy house, close the door, and shut out the openness.

The longest journey is the journey inward.

Afterword

Stephen O. Murray

My friend, who writes under the name Badruddin Khan, is by no means unanalytical about his cultural background, either in this book or elsewhere.[1] I tend to defer to "native" analyses, but he has nonetheless asked me to write something relating his book to social scientists' interests in using life histories as cultural data and in understanding homosexualities cross-culturally. Between these two topics, I have added a few remarks about migration and self-identification in a world in which someone can regularly fly from Toronto or London to Karachi in a day, as Badruddin does.

"In our own words"

Most of the occasions on which lesbians or gay men have described their worldview and lifeways "in their own words" for social scientists (including oral historians) have been shaped by questioners. Reading one particularly interesting attempt not to impose a pre-existing theoretical grid, Susan Krieger's *The Mirror Dance*, I wanted each of the characters who were blurred together as pieces in the author's analytical mosaic to be able to tell her own story, in her own order. Failing that, I wanted to

---

[1] Khan 1990; Murray and Khan in press and in conversation.

know what questions elicited responses that were then paraphrased in an alienating third person, and the order of the snippets that had been extracted for each informant. I also felt this way about the rich oral history materials in *Gay New York*, and even in *Boots of Leather, Slippers of Gold*.[1] I had more sense of some particular narrators in these histories than in Krieger's ethnography, and was reassured by Kennedy and Davis that they had not rearranged material *within* particular quotations.[2] Nonetheless they (mostly) omitted their questions. The "dialogue" in these books is between the analysis and the quotations the analysts selected and arranged, not between interviewers and those interviewed.[3] The same is true of the life histories in *Honey, Honey, Miss Thang* (Pettiway 1996).

As Dell Hymes has repeatedly argued,[4] vernacular "native" texts are open to reinterpretation by subsequent generations of scholars,[5] and also to reappropriation by subsequent generations of natives. The latter is particularly important in cases where direct cultural transmission is impaired by rapid social change,

---

[1] Chauncey 1994; Kennedy and Davis 1993; and to a lesser extent Marcus 1992.

[2] Kennedy and Davis 1993:397-8.

[3] Such control ("You talk, I decide what is important and publish it") is typical of cultural anthropology and qualitative sociology (see Mintz 1975; Clifford 1982; Murray 1983). Kennedy and Davis are among the least egregious practitioners of wrapping what they say in professional authority (cf. those criticized by Hong 1994a,b). In their book, Kennedy and Davis recorded interviewees' dissent from their interpretations (and also assent to them) more than most. They also presented their preliminary findings in community forums, are themselves more or less "natives," and are engaged in celebrating the agency of the people they studied. Even the most responsible ethnography is still a long way from real dialogue on the page, however.

[4] For example, Hymes 1965, 1983.

[5] For example, in Hymes 1981. See Darnell 1990.

hostility of a numerically superior dominant culture, and epidemic of early deaths.

To edit is to corrupt

Although I am an avid consumer of published life histories, I usually feel that, in compilations of lesbigay life histories, personal style has been edited out,[1] as I also feel in reading Native American "personal documents." I am in fervent agreement with what anthropologist Clyde Kluckhohn wrote about the classic Hopi life history, *Sun Chief*:[2] "The serious student wants to know at first-hand on what subjects the Hopi did tiresomely repeat himself. Every omission by the editor, every stylistic clarification takes us one more step away from what Don [the sun chief who wrote down his story] actually said."[3] I firmly believe that it is for the "natives" to decide what is important,[4] and that style of language *is* personality, not just an indicator or documentation of a personality.[5]

In the prolonged generation of this book, I have tried to keep myself from making suggestions about content. Besides

---

[1] For example, National Lesbian and Gay Survey 1993, Nardi *et al.* 1994.

[2] Simmons 1942.

[3] Kluckhohn 1943: 268; 1945:97. Also see Allport 1942:84.

[4] There is a whole other tradition, associated with ethnologists who were not accomplished ethnographers such as George Peter Murdock and Claude Lévi-Strauss. In a famous dismissal, the latter wrote: "For conscious models, which are usually known as 'norms,' are by definition very poor ones, since they are not intended to explain the phenomena but to perpetuate them" (Lévi-Strauss 1953: 527). In response to Hong (1994a), Lévi-Strauss (1994) denied that he rejected native models. Others who wrote to attack Hong (1994a) exemplified the smug view that "the analyst knows best and natives are poor deluded creatures, riddled with superstition and false consciousness." See Hong 1994b, pp. 26-27.

[5] See Sapir 1927; Friedrich and Redfield 1978. On the imperative of early American anthropology to collect "native texts," see Darnell 1990.

routine copyediting, I sometimes requested clarifications (so I am responsible to a considerable extent for the existence of most of the notes, though not for their content). I can recall four instances of suggesting topics that I thought were missing. Although I thought it was very interesting that Badruddin saw no need to explain how getting married in order to produce a child (preferably a son) was consistent with exclusively sheathed marital intercourse, I thought that the question was too interesting not to raise, and that it would occur to Muslim as well as non-Muslim readers. Badruddin addressed this issue briefly in a revision of his life story. He also responded briefly to my queries about his lack of any mention of any experiences or feelings of being discriminated against for being dark-skinned, Asian, and Muslim-named in North America. I am also responsible for raising the question of circumcision. Since it is universal to Pakistani males, he did not think to mention it—or to retrieve any particular memories about what is so taken for granted as to seem "natural." Badruddin either did not understand my question or ignored my asking about how and why the child fascinated with seizing penises grew up to be a "top." With these exceptions, the topics and incidents in the book are those he considered memorable and worth reporting.

Badruddin's sometimes perfumed style is unmistakably Persian/Urdu.[1] So, I think, are his rapier remarks that let in some fresh air when the reader is about to asphyxiate in some of the lyrical clouds of rhetoric about sexual partners' anatomy and physiology or other topics.

---

[1] See Naim 1979.

What kind of person exposes himself like this and why?

Besides cautioning against tampering with the native's words in "personal documents," Kluckhohn questioned what kind of native would produce such a document.[1] In cultures with the distrust of talk—especially talk to outsiders[2]—such volubility and self-display as is required to produce a life history raise questions about how typical the author of such a work is. In contrast, various observers have found openly gay men who are native speakers of English to be very willing to have their views and experiences reported[3]—to such an extent that hostile observers have quipped that "the love that didn't dare speak its name in the late 19th century won't shut up in the late 20th century." For an Anglo man, producing such a revealing "personal document" would not suggest deviance from one's culture as it does for a Native American. But discussing intimate details of family life, and particularly explicit accounts of sexual behavior (outside and—even more so—inside marriage), is very unusual for Muslims (and, more generally, Asians). Although, with this book, he obviously explodes out of his privacy container, Badruddin has lived his life in hyper-conformity to the cultural norm of keeping his feelings and any non-normative behavior secret. Even in telling his secrets here, he has been careful to establish an intermediary (me) who had to prove that he could protect the real name behind his pseudonym before he wrote about his own experiences.

---

[1] Kluckhohn 1943, 1945a:99, 138-45. Also see Kennedy and Davis 1993:18,24, which examines working-class women involved in the Buffalo gay bar scene of the 1940s and 1950s.

[2] See Basso 1970, Darnell 1981 on Native American non-talk.

[3] Including Leznoff 1956, Warren 1974.

Still, such a level of introspection remains unusual. As Badruddin notes, going through the motions of what is expected is *all* that is required. Islam is not a religion that encourages doubt and self-questioning.

Although there is a rich poetic/mystical tradition in Urdu (as in Persian, Arabic, and Turkish) employing the idiom of male love for a beautiful male,[1] feelings about loved ones (of any age or sex) were not recorded in Islamic fiction or nonfiction. As Grunebaum (who finds even poetry "unrevealing and discreet") noted:

> Even after the weakening of the classical ideal in the later Middle Ages, the biographer and especially the autobiographer dealt frankly and realistically only with religious development and to some extent with sensual enjoyment. Private experience is neither objectivized in action through novel or drama nor presented indirectly through the personification of virtues and ideas or through the casting of figures of history and legend to represent and express personal attitudes. There is abundant evidence for the Arab's keen understanding of man; but this is not to be found ... outside the religious sphere, in his confessional writing. (1952:332)[2]

---

[1] Murray 1996b discusses the inappropriateness of some of the characterizations for the supposed referent of Allah. On the specifically Urdu literature see Naim 1979.

[2] One should not infer from the absence of discourse and late development of the novel that there was no conception of a self. See Spiro (1993) on the general error of concluding non-Westerners do not conceive of selves, and Wikan (1990) for a refutation of the mistake in a specific place (predominantly Muslim north Bali).

Since World War II, there have been some North African novels in Arabic in which homosexual encounters and even persons generally known to be homosexual are represented, but there is no work of fiction or memoir that I know of that is written from within the subjectivity of a Muslim acting on a self-acknowledged homosexual preference.[1] This book is, therefore, a unique cultural document.

Badruddin makes no claims to be "typical" or "representative." Indeed, a recurrent topic in his life story is explaining what is conventional. He does not always know why he departed from conventions, but he knows what the conventions are. He points to examples of age-mates who made the accommodations he didn't, and relates some of the arguments they made in urging him to settle down to (re)producing a patriarchal unit of his own. He also knows there are alternative ways to live his life. He contrasts his own path of distancing himself from family and Pakistani communities to what he regards as the extreme path Haider took, cutting himself off from his natal family and depending entirely upon gay friends in North America, and to the attractively easier path that Aurangzeb took of settling down in Pakistan, marrying, siring children, and playing with male sexual partners on the side. Rather than succumbing to Anglo gay conformity (Haider) or Pakistani patriarchal surface conformity (Aurangzeb and Muhammed), Badruddin remained a patriarchal Muslim searching for submissive,

---

[1] See Murray (1996c:43-44) for a discussion of these other texts. Some of this North African fiction that is written in the first person recalls incidents of homosexual behavior, but not on the part of narrators who report feeling or having had desire—let alone a preference—for sex with other males. Moreover, some journalists in Pakistan have provided occasion for hustlers and *hijras* to say something about their lives (e.g., Mutjaba 1996; Naqvi and Mutjaba 1996).

pretty, young male partners among non-whites (Asians, Latinos, and Pacific Islanders) living in North America until recently, when he coupled with an Anglo-Canadian of roughly equivalent status. (I see status and age equivalence as more important than skin color, but other readers may differ in this interpretation.) Although he has for decades had Anglo gay friends (including myself), his hesitant moves toward involvement in the openly gay world were in gay Asian groups, mostly as a checkbook liberal—i.e., as a patron more than a participant—and he has scorned Anglo gay egalitarianism (in or out of the sheets). Perhaps there will be a sequel on adjusting to companionate marriage in North America!

The question remains why someone for whom discretion is so deeply ingrained would be motivated to undertake writing about his identities and sexual history. Trying to understand oneself is certainly one part of the motivation many of us have for writing, especially writing about ourselves.[1] Badruddin wanted to show why he is the way he is to sympathetic others, beginning with me. To do so, he was quite willing to expose aspects of himself that he knew would be judged negatively—some by other gay people, some by other Muslims, and perhaps some by most everyone. He is not unaware that many people will judge him harshly for having used dependents (family employees early on, later a wife). He tries to explain how he thought (or, more

---

[1] As Bourdieu (1987:2) puts it, "Autobiographical narrative is always at least partially motivated by a concern to give meaning, to rationalize . . . making oneself the ideologist of one's own life." I think that Bourdieu goes too far when he assumes that autobiographers turn reports of successive states "into steps of a necessary development": this is a possibility, but I do not see it actualized here, or in many other autobiographies. Even in narratives of religious conversion (e.g., Radin 1926), some contingency remains, and there is only a tendency to schematize a quasi-inevitable progression.

exactly, why it didn't occur to him to think about such ways of viewing his conduct).

Self-justification is a common motive, especially in political memoirs, but I do not think it was a very important one in this case. To some extent Badruddin was trying to explain to readers the reasonableness of his natal family's assumptions about religion, sex, and (what is most sacred to them) the family. Before undertaking to write about himself, he endeavored to explain the limited "tolerance"[1] for circumspect homosexual sex in urban Pakistan. He was irritated by "Western" representations of repression and intolerance in Islamic societies during the 1980s. In 1990, in an article he wrote, which I titled "Not-so-gay life in Karachi,"[2] he illustrated what Paul Kutsche calls an implicit "social contract" in which men can have sex with boys and men as long as no one talks about it and as long as family obligations are met. Badruddin's personal narrative shows his lived experience of the contract. He exhibits more than a little nostalgia for when he didn't know any better, but in breaking silence on such subjects, he challenges "the will not to know," which I see as the traditional Islamic tactic for containing any kind of sexual variance (not just male-male sex).[3]

---

[1] In regard to Latin America and Thailand, I have discussed how silence about homosexuality is certainly not positive valuation of it (Murray 1992, 1995a:33-64). Rather, silence is the upper limit of "tolerance" for *individual* desires. I believe that the same familial obstacles to gay life and identity occur in other cultures where the structural basis of a welfare society "safety net" is lacking and the establishment of gay institutions is literally unthinkable.
[2] Khan 1990.
[3] Kutsche 1995, Murray 1996c.

Staying Away and (Only Partial) "Westernization"

To me, the strongest evidence of the durability of his natal culture's continued channeling of Badruddin's feeling and thinking is what seems to be the non sequitur that Haider "died alone" surrounded by friends. Doesn't "alone" mean with no one else present? Not within Badruddin's cultural assumptions. Only the family counts, so culturally "surrounded by friends" is still "alone," and this is a meaningful statement, not a non sequitur. In the pages that follow (pages 137-144), Badruddin's horror at being completely cut off from his family is palpable, as he strives unsuccessfully to be analytical. He blames the death on Haider's cutting himself off, not on the proximate cause: his failing to have safe, or at least, protected sex.

That he never specifically decided to stay in North America is also interesting. I think that much of the literature on human migration assumes rational cost-benefit analysis. As Alden Speare noted, "The biggest problem with the application of a cost-benefit model to human migration may not be the crudeness of the actual calculation, but the fact that many people never make any calculation at all."[1]

Are you "what you do" to earn a living?

Although I am somewhat dubious of the utility of the concept of "personality," especially as a constant entity,[2] I think Badruddin demonstrates a continuity of viewpoint both with what he says about his childhood and adolescence and from situation to situation. His narrative reports only some of his roles and

---

[1] 1971:130. For an exemplary study of the complex postmodern movement forth and back and forth see Massey *et al.* 1987.

[2] See Murray 1986a,b; Bourdieu 1987; Spiro 1993.

relations, mostly those in his natal family, plus in friendships and sexual relations in Pakistan and in North America.

Conspicuous by their absence is mention of work associates, work life, or even any clear indication of exactly what Baddruddin's occupation is. In North America, as he certainly knows, what you do is frequently regarded as equivalent to who you are. Badruddin's "real life" is so segregated from his work life, that it does not occur to him to mention the latter. When my life partner—who is from another very family-oriented culture in which personal feelings are not discussed (even inside the family)—first met Badruddin, he was struck by the evasiveness of Badruddin's response (definitely not an answer!) to the "What do you do [for a living]?" question, and, ever since then, has regarded him as pathologically secretive—in particular, as not confiding anything to those he auditions for the role of "beloved."[1] Although Badruddin and I speak on the phone often, I have never known Badruddin's work phone number(s). He is also the only person I know with "personal" checks that do not include an address or a phone number. Although he wrote this book, he definitely is not one who shares his feelings promiscuously or lets very many people know about his relationships, his desires, or his frustrations. Work is work, home is home and never the twain shall meet!

---

[1] Although he does not make the lover/beloved contrast (using the North American generic "lover"), it seems applicable: He clearly has been the lover, frustrated by attractive but fickle beloveds who escape his control and fail to devote themselves to serv[ic]ing him in ways echoing the Islamic "martyr to love" literature (see Giffen 1971:99-115).

Childhood effeminacy and the egalitarian ("gay") reorganization of homosexuality

I want to conclude my remarks by using *Sex, Longing & Not Belonging* to address two major topics in the study of homosexuality: the childhood effeminacy explanation for male homosexuality and the evolution from status-defined to egalitarian homosexuality.

American gay men recall feeling different at an early age, often before having any notion of the mechanics of sex or much of any sense of gender conventions.[1] About half recall childhood gender nonconformity—which means that half do not.[2] Many of the latter still recall the feeling of being outside, observing rather than unself-consciously participating in normal boys' life. The sickly child, Badruddin, was one of these. He read a lot and did not play sports. As an adult he has little interest in spectator sports, though he works out at a gym and is masculine in his self-presentation. I would not conclude much from a sample of one, but it is at least interesting that he reports the same pattern of early sensing of difference and estrangement from what seemed natural family life and male activity. Although he periodically claims to have given up the security of being enveloped in family (e.g., claiming that "when I was growing up in Pakistan. I *belonged*"), it is clear that he was an

---

[1] More than do lesbians: see Whisman 1995.

[2] See Harry 1982. There is a strong, statistically significant difference between the recollected childhood gender conformity of gay and straight men, though the extent is probably exaggerated to some degree by adult models of what one should have been like as a child (so that gay men and their parents and siblings are more likely to remember and are more often reminded of childhood gender deviance and straight men have repressed or suppress any such memories. For a prospective study of especially effeminate boys, see Green 1986.

outsider in his own natal family, mostly raised by his grandmother, lacking intimacy with his father, his siblings, and even his mother. Attraction to males was not what first set him apart in his own mind: the constraints imposed on a sickly child were.

There is no evidence that he considered himself effeminate or was considered effeminate by others or called names such as *gandu*. In Pakistan, a man's role is to sire children to extend patrilines. It is precisely this that Badruddin has failed to do, and there is a sense in which any male who has failed to reproduce is a specimen of failed masculinity.[1] So, if he lived as an adult in Pakistan, Badruddin's masculinity might be questioned (and/or it might be assumed that his long stay in the West "spoiled" it in some way that would be better not to speculate about!).

Longing to belong is the leitmotif of Badruddin's memoir. The family's nominal faith provided no sense of secure belonging.[2] Badruddin felt estranged to some degree from the family itself, which he recognizes (and recognized) was the central institution of Pakistani society. He was not satisfied to partake of the "social contract" that peripheralizes male-male sexual relations

---

[1] I think that this generic category of nonprocreative males has been confused by the narrower physiological sense of "impotence" in English translation of South Asian texts. On subcategorizations of nonprocreative males in pre-Mughal South Asia, see Sweet and Zwilling 1993.

[2] In this, he is quite similar to Shahid, the protagonist of Hanif Kureishi's (1995) novel, *The Black Album*. The second son of a successful Pakistani immigrant family, Shahid grew up in England in a totally secular household. When he tells his sister-in-law that he has been to the local mosque, "she pretended her legs were giving way [and said], 'But you had a decent upbringing!'" (p. 198). Shahid longs to belong, but after flirting with Islamicism opts for Western sex (specifically, sex with an English woman).

even while allowing them to exist on the peripheries.[1] In North America he resisted being defined as "Asian"[2] or "Pakistani" or "gay."

Given the importance to him of his quest for a male beloved, his rejection of gay identity and of the gay label will puzzle many Western gay readers who see it as more or less "natural" to come out, to socialize with other gay men, and to participate in the gay communities that have been growing and providing more and more services overtly for gay men.[3]

It seems to me that Badruddin was seeking homo-love, homo-sex being readily available—in his view almost too readily available.[4] Like more than a few natives of Anglo North Amer-

---

[1] I do not mean to claim that the sole reason for not returning to Pakistan was sexual. As socially elite as his family is in Pakistan, his (hard currency) income has been higher working in North America. The levels of street violence and religious pressure are also much lower in Toronto than in Karachi. Where one lives has multiple determinants, not all of them conscious.

[2] He does not examine (let alone define) this category in his memoir, but has told me that "Asian" means Confucian (East Asian-West Pacific: China, Korea, Japan, Taiwan, the latter two being Pacific islands) to Canadians and Americans, not least to "Asian-Canadians" and "Asian-Americans."

[3] See Murray 1996a:182-214. Badruddin does not mention the tradition of Sufi mystics who often seem to be in love with Love (Love and God being indistinguishable). The explicit intertextuality involves American psychiatrists and the novels of Jean Genet and Gore Vidal. The rejection of being identified with a stigmatizing label is close to Vidal's, however based it is in the irreality of nonprocreation in Pakistan. The very Protestant individualism and quest for authenticity of André Gide's journals and memoir (*Si le grain ne meurt*) which spoke to me before I had any homosexual experience probably would not have spoken to Badruddin even if he had read them. (He only mentions reading Gide's *Corydon*, which is much less concerned with standing out and being counted than with arguing that being used sexually is good for young males.)

[4] Somewhere James Baldwin said that sex and money are only important to those who do not have them (admittedly many people). Like Baldwin, Bad-

(*continued . . .*)

ica, he found the ready provision of sex (not only impersonal sex) more an obstacle than a path to love. He does not think that his attitude toward his sexual partners was instrumental, but I think that *Sex, Longing & Not Belonging* shows the obdurateness of status-defined homosexuality at the intrapsychic level. The young Badruddin grabbed the penises of servants who were afraid to resist the master's son's demands. The adult Badruddin's sexual career has almost exclusively consisted of taking the insertive role in sex with younger, less masculine, and less affluent partners (i.e., combinations of three "inferior" statuses). Although now attempting an egalitarian relationship (with a smooth and slight white/Anglo bottom), he has no real experience with equality in a relationship. Even in his current relationship, he has a considerable "edge" when it comes to income, formal education, physical size, and age.[1] That is his current adventure, and interested readers will have to wait for a sequel about the success or failure of that adjustment!

(. . . continued)
ruddin has been searching for mutual love (generally without the sexual reciprocation that is normative but not invariant in "modern gay" homosexuality—see Murray 1996a:2).

[1] In reviewing studies of American gay couples, I found that "perceived equality in decision-making is not necessarily lacking in couples who differ substantially in age, status, or income; but the older and/or more affluent partner tends to dominate decision-making in such relationships" (Murray 1996a:171). Carrington (1997) shows that the lesbian or gay partner who takes more responsibility in the domestic sphere tends to feel effeminized, though the less domestic partner often tries to exaggerate egalitarianism in the relationship and to shore up the status of the partner (often denying that domestic responsibilities "feminize" their partner) when representing their relationship to others. Moreover, hairiness (facial and body) is a gender marker among males in Pakistan, as in other Muslim societies.

References

Allport, Gordon. 1942. *The Use of Personal Documents in Psychological Science*. New York: Social Science Research Council.

Basso, Keith H. 1970. "To give up on words": Silence in Western Apache culture. *Southwestern Journal of Anthropology* 26:213-230.

Bourdieu, Pierre. 1986. L'illusion biographique. *Actes de la recherche en sciences sociales* 62/63:69-72. English translation by Yves Winkin and Wendy Leeds-Hurwitz, *Working Papers and Proceedings of the Center for Psychosocial Studies* [Chicago] 14, 1987.

Bruner, Jerome. 1990. *Acts of Meaning*. Cambridge, MA: Harvard University Press.

Carrington, Christopher. 1997. *Lesbian and Gay Couples' Domestic and Emotional Labor*. Ph.D. dissertation, University of Massachusetts, Amherst.

Chauncey, George. 1994. *Gay New York*. New York: Basic Books.

Clifford, James. 1982. Fieldwork, reciprocity and the making of ethnographic texts. *Man* 15:518-521.

Darnell, Regna D. 1981. Taciturnity in Native American Etiquette: A Cree case. *Culture* 1:55-60.

———. 1990. Franz Boas, Edward Sapir, and the Americanist text tradition. *Historiographia Linguistica* 17:129-144.

Dollard, John. 1935. *Criteria for the Life History*. New Haven: Yale University Press.

Fischer, Michael M. J. 1986. Ethnicity and the post-modern arts of memory. Pp. 194-233 in J. Clifford and G. Marcus, *Writing Culture*. Berkeley: University of California Press.

Friedrich, Paul, and James Redfield. 1978. Speech as a personality symbol: The case of Achilles. *Language* 54:263-288.

Giffen, Lois Anita. 1971. *Theory of Profane Love among the Arabs: The Development of the Genre*. New York: New York University Press.

Green, Richard. 1986. *Sissy Boys Grow Up*. New Haven, CT: Yale University Press.

Grunebaum, Gustave E. von. 1948. The nature of the Arabic literary effort. *Journal of Near Eastern Studies* 4:116-121.

———. 1952. The aesthetic foundation of Arabic literature. *Comparative Literature* 4:323-340.

Harry, Joseph. 1982. *Gay Children Grow Up*. New York: Praeger.

Hong, Keelung. 1994a. Experiences of being a 'native' observing anthropologists. *Anthropology Today* 10,3:6-9.

———. 1994b. Reply. *Anthropology Today* 10,5:26-27.

Hymes, Dell H. 1965. Some North Pacific Coast poems." *American Anthropologist* 67:316-341.
———. 1981. *"In Vain I Tried to Tell You": Essays in Native American Ethnopoetics.* Philadelphia: University of Pennsylvania Press.
———. 1983. *Studies in the History of Linguistics.* Amsterdam: John Benjamins.
Kennedy, Elizabeth Lapovsky, and Madeline D. Davis. 1993. *Boots of Leather, Slippers of Gold: The History of a Lesbian Community.* New York: Routledge.
Khan, Badruddin. 1990. Not-so-gay life in Karachi. *Society of Lesbian and Gay Anthropologists' Newsletter* 12,1:10-19. Revised version in *Islamic Homosexualities.* by Stephen Murray and Will Roscoe, 275-296. New York: New York University Press.
Kluckhohn, Clyde. 1943. Review of Simmons (1942). *American Anthropologist* 45:267-270.
———. 1945a. The personal document in anthropological science. *Social Science Research Council Bulletin* 53:79-173.
———. 1945b. A Navaho personal document with a brief paretian analysis. *Southwest Journal of Anthropology* 1:260-283.
Krieger, Susan. 1983. *The Mirror Dance.* Philadelphia: Temple University Press.
Kureishi, Hanif. 1995. *The Black Album.* New York: Scribner.
Kutsche, Paul. 1995. Two truths about Costa Rica. In *Latin American Male Homosexualities* by Stephen Murray, 111-137. Albuquerque: University of New Mexico Press.
Lévi-Strauss, Claude. 1953. Social structure. In *Anthropology Today,* ed. by Alfred Kroeber, 524-553. Chicago: University of Chicago Press.
———. 1994. Comment on Hong (1994). *Anthropology Today* 10,5: in press.
Leznoff, Maurice. 1956. Interviewing homosexuals. *American Journal of Sociology* 62:202-204.
Mandelbaum, David. 1973. The study of life history. *Current Anthropology* 14:177-206.
Marcus, Eric. 1992. *Making History: The Struggle for Gay and Lesbian Equal Rights.* New York: HarperCollins.
Massey, Douglas S., Rafael Alarcón, Jorge Durand, and Humberto González. 1987. *Return to Aztlán: The Social Process of International Migration from Western Mexico.* Berkeley: University of California Press.
Mintz, Sidney. 1979. The anthropological interview and the life history. *Oral History Review* 7:18-26.
Murray, Stephen O. 1983. The creation of linguistic structure. *American Anthropologist* 85:356-362.
———. 1986a. Chicago studies of language and personality. *History of Sociology* 6,2:75-108.

———. 1986b. Edward Sapir in 'the Chicago School of sociology.' In *New Perspectives in Language, Culture, and Personality: Proceedings of the Sapir Centenary Conference*, ed. by Konrad Koerner et al., 241-291. Amsterdam: John Benjamins.

———. 1992. The "underdevelopment" of gay homosexuality in urban Mesoamerica, Peru and Thailand. In *Modern Homosexualities* ed. by Ken Plummer, 29-38. London: Routledge.

———. 1995a. *Latin American Male Homosexualities*. Albuquerque: University of New Mexico Press.

———. 1995b. Stigma transformation and relexification in the international diffusion of *gay*. In *Beyond the Lavender Lexicon: Gay and Lesbian Language*. ed. by William Leap, 236-260. New York: Gordon & Breach.

———. 1996a. *American Gay*. Chicago: University of Chicago Press.

———. 1996b. Corporealizing medieval Persian and Turkish tropes. In *Islamic Homosexualities* by Stephen Murray and Will Roscoe, 132-141. New York: New York University Press.

———. 1996c. The will not to know: Islamic accommodations of male homosexuality. In *Islamic Homosexualities* by Stephen Murray and Will Roscoe, 14-54. New York: New York University Press.

Murray, Stephen O., and Badruddin Khan. in press. Keeping male-male sexual relations invisible in Pakistan. To appear in *Male Homosexuality Around the World*, ed. by Donald West and Richard Green. New York: Plenum.

Mutjaba, Hasan. 1996. "The other side of midnight": Pakistani male prostitutes. In *Islamic Homosexualities* by Stephen Murray and Will Roscoe, 267-274. New York: New York University Press.

Naim, C. M. 1979. The theme of homosexual (pederastic) love in pre-modern Urdu poetry. In *Studies in Urdu Gazal and Prose Fiction*, ed. by Umar Memon, 120-142. Madison: University of Wisconsin Press.

Naqvi, Nauman, and Hasan Mujtaba. 1996. Two Baluchi *buggas*, a Sindhi *zenana*, and the status of *hijras* in contemporary Pakistan. In *Islamic Homosexualities* by Stephen Murray and Will Roscoe, 262-266. New York: New York University Press.

Nardi, Peter M., David Sanders, and Judd Marmor. 1994. *Growing Up Before Stonewall: Life Stories of Some Gay Men*. New York: Routledge.

National Lesbian and Gay Survey. 1993. *Proust, Cole Porter, Michelangelo, Marc Almond and Me: Writings by Gay Men on Their Lives and Lifestyles*. New York: Routledge.

Pettiway, Leon F. 1996. *Honey, Honey, Miss Thang: Being Black, Gay, and on the Streets*. Philadelphia: Temple University Press.

Plummer, Kenneth. 1983. *Documents of Life*. London: Allen & Unwin.

———. 1994. *Telling Sexual Stories*. New York: Routledge.
Radin, Paul. 1926. *The Autobiography of a Winnebago Indian*. New York: Dover.
Sapir, Edward. 1927. Speech as a personality trait. *American Journal of Sociology* 32:892-905.
Simmons, Leo. 1942. *Sun Chief*. New Haven: Yale University Press.
Speare, Alden, Jr. 1971. A cost-benefit model of rural to urban migration in Taiwan. *Population Studies* 25:117-130.
Spiro, Melford E. 1993. Is the Western conception of the self "peculiar" within the context of world cultures?" *Ethos* 21:107-153.
Sweet, Michael J., and Leonard Zwilling. 1993. The first medicalization: The taxonomy and etiology of queerness in classical Indian medicine. *Journal of the History of Sexuality* 3:590-607.
Warren, Carol A. B. 1974. *Identity and Community in the Gay World*. New York: Wiley.
Whisman, Vera. 1995. *Queer by Choice*. New York: Routledge.
Wikan, Unni. 1990. *Managing Turbulent Hearts: A Balinese Formula for Living*. Chicago: University of Chicago Press.